YORK NOTES

General Editors: Professor A.N. Jeff
of Stirling) & Professor Suheil Bushr
University of Beirut)

George Bernard Shaw

THE DEVIL'S DISCIPLE

Notes by Emelie FitzGibbon

MA B MUS H DIP ED (NUI)
Tutor in English,
University College of Cork, Ireland

LONGMAN
YORK PRESS

YORK PRESS
Immeuble Esseily, Place Riad Solh, Beirut.

LONGMAN GROUP LIMITED
Longman House,
Burnt Mill,
Harlow,
Essex

© Librairie du Liban 1985

First published 1985
ISBN 0 582 79262 2
Printed in Hong Kong by
Sheck Wah Tong Printing Press Ltd

Contents

Part 1

Introduction

The age of George Bernard Shaw

The keynote of the years from 1855 to 1950 was change, possibly the most rapid social, political and artistic change the world has ever known. When Shaw was born in 1856 Victoria (1819–1901) was still queen of a British Empire which held dominion over much of the world; life for the aristocratic and monied classes was leisured and cultivated while life for the millions of poor workers was nasty, brutish and short; education was a privilege which relatively few could afford; art favoured sentimental and patriotic themes; morality was strict and religious observation socially obligatory. When Shaw died this world had been shattered by two violent wars and had seen the atomic bombing of Hiroshima and Nagasaki; radically altered economic and social conditions had ensured a more even distribution of wealth; the development of mass communications media had changed expectations and had ensured the speedy dissemination of knowledge; education was available to all classes; orthodox religious observation was on the decline, and art had utterly rejected the forms and themes of the earlier century.

What caused this acceleration of change in the settled patterns of life, in modes of behaviour, economic and social affairs, political ideologies and artistic tastes? In the first place, the growth of large urban areas with industries which employed workers for regular and limited hours led to an increase of leisure time for the ordinary man or woman, time to consider and to think; it led to the possibility that large numbers of like-minded people could congregate for meetings; it ensured the death of the old feudal responsibilities where commitment to the lord and the land were one and, consequently, it led to a new independence of the working man. As a result of this, there emerged a greater awareness of the political power of the worker, a development of trade unionism and an increasingly efficient agitation for governmental action in the areas of education, health and social welfare. Secondly, growth of the means of inexpensive mass communication in newspapers, radio and, at the end of the era, television, led to more a widespread appreciation of social and political affairs and to a corresponding increase in sophistication of the electorate. The now powerful and informed voter knew not to believe everything he heard from politicians but believed in his right to hear as wide a range of opinions as possible. Finally, the cataclysmic disaster of the first World War changed not only the national boundaries of the world but also its mental and social ones. The loss of so many of the officer class broke up the great landed estates with their settled and unquestioned class structure; women who, for the duration of the war, had worked in men's occupations were not content to return to their former subordinate role but sought suffrage, equality and independence; returning soldiers, finding themselves unemployed labourers rather than welcomed heroes, turned militantly against the system which had rejected them; and, perhaps most important of all, the mental insecurity caused by a war which had altered the entire world had far-reaching effects not only on its frenetic survivors in the Twenties Jazz Age and the Thirties dole queues but also on the next generation which was itself torn apart by another global war. This world of change from the secure values and patterns of Victorian life to the insecurity of possible atomic destruction was the world of George Bernard Shaw.

It was in the social and political spheres that the change was at its most rapid in the latter part of the era. Up to the turn of the century, despite growing agitation for reform, there was minimal change in the British class system. Each class was rigidly defined, had its own forms of cohesion and its own rules of behaviour. This rigidity allowed for very little social mobility, and only the growth of an economically independent middle class disturbed the almost feudal relationship between the landed gentry and their servants. For the upper classes this was an age of gold; a personal account of the London 'season' of the late 1880s describes how

> In the afternoon it was *de rigeur* to drive on the Knightsbridge side of the Park. There the carriageway would present an almost solid phalanx of victorias, barouches, and landaus [coaches], all with coachmen and footmen, many of them powdered. In them sat elaborately dressed and *coiffured* women and their daughters, *les jeunes filles à marier*. Up and down they drove for the regulation number of turns, bowing to their friends and trying to look as if they were enjoying themselves. Women not quite in the swim tried to look as if they were; in the seventh heaven if someone belonging to the inner circle gave them a careless half-bow.*

At the other end of the social spectrum, however, poverty imposed harsh conditions on the vast numbers of urban poor. As late as 1903, the writer Jack London (1876–1916) went to experience life in the London slums: his descriptions differ little from those given fifty years

* Percy Coulson, *Close of an Era: 1887–1914*, Hutchinson, London, 1945.

before by Charles Dickens (1812−70). In the slums and tenements men and women worked in the 'sweated trades'; that is, trades in which people, in fierce competition for the available work, laboured in their own homes, with their own equipment, to produce the required goods at the lowest possible price. In *People of the Abyss* (1903), London and his guide went to visit a place of sweated labour:

> Up we went, three flights, each landing two feet by three in area, and heaped with filth and rubbish . . . . In six of the rooms, twenty-odd people of both sexes and all ages cooked, ate, slept and worked. In size the rooms averaged eight feet by eight, or possibly nine. The seventh room we entered. It was seven feet wide by eight long, and the table at which the work [shoemaking] was performed took up the major portion of that space . . . . My sweated friend, when work was to be had, toiled with four other men in his eight by seven room. In the winter a lamp burned nearly all day and added its fumes to the overloaded air, which was breathed, and breathed and breathed again.

Such extreme discrepancies of ways of living, behaviour and expectations were, however, coming to an end. The word 'unemployed' first appeared in the *Oxford English Dictionary* in 1881, and it was the unemployed, workers with no social legislation to keep them from utter poverty and destitution, who provided a fertile ground for the growth of a Labour movement which sought to secure employment at a living wage for all who needed it and social welfare acts to protect those unfortunate enough to lose that employment. Sporadic social reforms in the 1890s provided the impetus for further reforms and the coming to power of a Liberal government in 1906 accelerated the process of parliamentary and social change. Far-reaching strikes in 1911 and 1913, while they failed in their immediate purposes, nevertheless showed that the new power of the working man could not be ignored with impunity, particularly when that same working man was required to give his life for king and country in the years to follow.

Britain entered the war on 4 August, 1914. It was confidently predicted that this would be a limited war, it 'would be over by Christmas', and none of the combatants in their worst nightmares envisaged the devastating conflict it was to become. Casualties were severe: approximately ten million were killed and the unseen 'casualties' of civilians, war widows and orphans, were many times that number. It was a war which combined the bravura and the military techniques of a lost age with the horrors of modern warfare: saturation shelling with ever more destructive weapons and, in the form of mustard gas, chemical warfare. Nobody who survived such a war could be untouched by its waste, horror and futility, and the laudable aim of the

British Prime Minister to create 'a country fit for heroes to live in' echoed hollowly in the atmosphere of cynicism and apathy which followed the end of hostilities. The measure of the change from feelings of high patriotism to a detached posture of cynical indifference can, perhaps, best be taken from an observation of the different attitudes of the war poets. Rupert Brooke (1887–1915), who volunteered for active service (a commissioned officer, he died of fever at Skyros, on his way to the Dardanelles), expressed the grandeur of the early feelings of patriotism, while the later writings of Wilfred Owen (1893–1918) and Siegfried Sassoon (1886–1967), with their acknowledgement of the stupidity of the war, showed how disillusionment with the war effort increased as the years of its destruction wore on. The cynics, it would seem, were right; the war machine survived by its own efforts. On 3 September 1939 the 'land fit for heroes to live in' once again declared war, this time on Hitler's Germany. The first World War (1914–18) 'the war to end all wars', had failed in its primary objective but, inadvertently, succeeded in bringing sweeping social change in its wake; the autocratic, conservative governments which were seen as the perpetrators of the war were rejected in favour of newer, more radical approaches to social organisation.

The economically based theories of Karl Marx (1818–83), which were voiced in his major works *The Communist Manifesto* (1848) and *Das Kapital* (1867), developed into the political philosophies of Socialism and Communism and altered many working men's views of themselves as entities in the system of government. Russia was the first country to change Marxist doctrines from political theory to political practice when the overthrow of the oppressive Tsarist regime in 1917 created a new Communist state. The Russian Revolution caused a sharp divergence of opinion among socialists in Britain, most of whom admired the theory of the new state but deplored the violence used in achieving it. However, change in Britain's social organisation was seen to be necessary and the modified forms of socialism favoured both by the emerging Labour party and such intellectual groups as Shaw's Fabians (who sought gradual social change—without violence) brought about, if not a social revolution, at least the progressive democratisation of government and the movement of all political parties away from conservatism towards a newer concept of social democracy.

Conservative artistic stances, too, were undermined by those who were intent on proclaiming the supremacy of individual vision. While Sigmund Freud (1856–1939) demonstrated how much of man's behaviour was determined by the patterns he made for himself in his mind, artists such as the Impressionists and Post-Impressionists—for example, Claude Monet (1840–1926), Pierre Renoir (1841–1919), Vincent Van Gogh (1853–90) and Paul Cezanne (1839–1906) demonstrated how the patterns man perceived in the world around him were determined by patterns of light and shade on the retina of his eye, and sought to create paintings based on these impressions of colour. According to Monet 'light is the principal person in the picture', and he and the other artists abandoned naturalistic depiction of scenes in favour of painting strong patterns of colour and light.

Individuality ruled perception, thought and expression. In art, formal concepts of line, perspective and realistic reproduction were rejected in favour of individualistic perception. In poetry, formal concepts of metrics, poetic diction and standard verse forms were rejected in favour of sharply individualistic images expressed in a language far removed from ornament and cliché: *The Waste Land* (1922) by T.S. Eliot (1888–1965) is perhaps the greatest poem in this Imagist style. In prose, the form of straightforward narrative was shattered by the use made of the 'stream of consciousness' technique by James Joyce (1882–1941). And in drama, romantic comedy and melodrama were challenged by the social drama of Henrik Ibsen (1828–1906), the acting practice of Konstantin Stanislavsky (1865–1938) and the design theories of Gordon Craig (1872–1966) and Adolf Appia (1862–1924). Among novelists Arnold Bennett (1867–1931), Thomas Hardy (1840–1928), John Galsworthy (1867–1933), all traditional writers, commanded a much wider public than did the innovators. In retrospect, however, we can see that it was the innovators, the iconoclasts, who gave most accurate expression to this age when the old moulds were broken, and in the swirling vortex of constant uncertainty and change no new moulds could be formed.

The life of George Bernard Shaw

George Bernard Shaw was born in Dublin, Ireland, on 26 July 1856, the last child and only son of George Carr Shaw and Lucinda Elizabeth Gurley. On his father's side he laid claim to descent from the Scottish hero, Macduff, and, while this claim was later disproved, it was at least true that the family came originally from Scotland, probably to fight with King William's forces against the Jacobite rebels of 1690. On his mother's side, he was descended from a line of small landowners, Protestant and Unionist in sympathies and respectable in social standing. George Carr Shaw, however, despite his own respectable ancestry, seems to have been ineffectual both as father and as husband, and the marriage ended in 1871 with Elizabeth's departure for London, accompanied by her two daughters. His father's financial ineptitude no less than his alcoholism meant that George Bernard Shaw grew up, if not in poverty, then in circumstances of genteel impoverishment. Yet in his early life financial security was not a primary motivating force, and in 1856, after five years in trade as a messenger-boy and clerk, Shaw left the financial security of eighty pounds a year to join his mother in London and begin the traditionally precarious career of a writer.

His first significant employment was secured through the good offices of George Vandaleur Lee, his mother's former singing teacher. On being asked to become music critic for the newspaper *The Hornet*, Lee accepted, but asked Shaw to 'ghost' the articles for him; that is to write the articles but to allow Lee to get the credit for them. Nonetheless, even at the princely sum of a guinea (twenty one shillings; in contemporary coinage one pound and five pence) per article, writing reviews never kept anyone alive for very long and Shaw gradually became known as a tall shabby eccentric attending concerts and operas in old, 'unsuitable' clothes. Sartorial elegance, however, did not appear to Shaw to be essential for a writer; and the notoriety he gained both by his criticism and by his eccentric appearance made him a recognisable figure in the London literary world. Recognition was not all he acquired. Writing the reviews for Lee had given Shaw a taste for the intoxicating richness of words; training himself to read music, to follow the scores of the great operas, had inculcated in him a love of sound and structure; observing the foibles of his family, his acquaintances, and, not least, himself had sharpened his skills. The time was ripe for him to begin writing at greater length.

In March 1879 he began to write a novel, *Immaturity*. It was rejected by several publishers, but with the optimism of youth Shaw immediately embarked on another novel. It, too, was rejected, as were his third, fourth and fifth efforts and in 1885 he gave up novel writing; by then his interests lay in other areas. It was in 1882 that there occurred three events which were to have a significant effect on Shaw's career: he strayed by chance into a meeting addressed by the American socialist, Henry George (1839–97), and, according to himself, the speech he heard 'changed the whole current of [his] life'; in the British Museum he read Marx's *Das Kapital* which consolidated his socialist thought and provided him with a basis for his philosophy; he made the acquaintance of the journalist and translator of Ibsen's plays, William Archer (1856–1924), who was then drama critic for *The World*. Shaw's conversion to socialist politics and the theatre, the twin passions of his long life, had begun.

At the instigation of Archer, Shaw wrote his first play, *Widowers' Houses*, in 1884. However, it was substantially rewritten in 1892 after Shaw discovered in Archer's translations of the plays of Henrik Ibsen the dramatic voice he had been seeking. In Ibsen's plays he found a reforming zeal and a didactic insistence which matched his own, and their example, together with his own flair for ironic dialogue, led to the development of Shaw's characteristic style. *The Philanderer* (1893) and *Mrs Warren's Profession* (1893) followed in rapid succession, although the latter was banned by the censor because it dealt with the profits made from prostitution. His fourth play, the anti-heroic comedy, *Arms and the Man* (1894), was the first to achieve a public showing, and it demonstrated to Shaw that in sharp comedy lay his greatest weapon: comedy need not be trivial or unintellectual but can sometimes sustain a didactic message more effectively than tragedy. So, while Shaw's puritanical reforming self urged drama of serious social issues, his pragmatic self did not ignore the popular forms of his day and the undoubted box-office appeal of comedy and melodrama. The melodrama *The Devil's Disciple* (1896–7) gave Shaw his first commercial success when it was performed in New York in 1897 with the popular American actor, Richard Mansfield, in the title role. In 1898, Shaw earned over two thousand five hundred pounds from the production and promptly abandoned all his journalistic pursuits to devote himself entirely to drama and to his socialist commitments. It was in 1898 also that Shaw, at the age of forty-three, married his 'Irish millionairess', the wealthy heiress, Charlotte Payne Townshend (1857–1943).

Despite his American triumph, Shaw's plays were still not acceptable to English theatre managements, and though play followed play in quick succession—*Candida* (1894), *You Never Can Tell* (1896), *Caesar and Cleopatra* (1898), *Captain Brassbound's Conversion* (1899)—it was not until 1904 that they achieved any real recognition as anything other than published play texts, read by a select minority of theatregoers. In 1904 J.E. Vedrenne (1867–1930) and H. Granville Barker (1877–1946) decided to use the Royal Court Theatre in Sloane Square, London, for a season of 'intellectual modern plays' which were, as yet, unacceptable to commercial managements. *Candida* was performed for a few matinées and a new Shaw play, *John Bull's Other Island* (1904), followed. The next year another new play, *Major Barbara* (1905), was staged, as was a production of *You Never Can Tell*, and a further new play, *Man and Superman* (1901–3) which ran for a record 176 performances. Shaw's fortunes had turned and the commercial as well as artistic success of his subsequent plays was assured. In the years that followed the imaginative range and power of his plays continued to expand: *Pygmalion* (1912), *Heartbreak House* (performed 1919), the epic *Back to Methuselah* (1921), *Saint Joan* (1923) and *The Apple Cart* (1929) were foremost among his later works. In all, Shaw wrote fifty-seven plays, the last, *Buoyant Billions*, was finished in 1948, when Shaw was ninety-three.

His work in drama, however, great though it was, formed only a part of the complex total personality of George Bernard Shaw. Shaw held strongly, and publicly expressed, opinions about everything: social conditions, politics, war, and religion, the function of art, vegetarianism and vivisection. And he was not an idle theorist but sought, in a way of living which was ascetic despite the wealth amassed by his wife and himself, to practise what he preached. As a convinced socialist, he became a leading member of the Fabians and frequently spoke at public meetings on the need for social reform. In accord with Fabian policy, he thought that this reform could be achieved not by a revolt by the working classes but by gradual reform enunciated and achieved by the educated. 'The real secret of Marx's fascination', Shaw wrote in the magazine *The Candid Friend* (1901), 'was his appeal to an unnamed, unrecognized passion: the hatred in the more generous souls among the respectable and educated sections for middle-class institutions that had starved, thwarted, misled and corrupted them spiritually from their cradles'. Chief among these spiritually corrupting institutions were the great world religions which sought to impose a single system of beliefs on all their adherents. Shaw saw all religions as fundamentally deceptive, promising a spurious salvation in an after-life but ignoring the conditions in which man endured his life on earth.

George Bernard Shaw died at Ayot St Lawrence in England on 2 November 1950. His disposition of his estate, which was exceptionally large for a writer, was typical of the complex and multifaceted man that Shaw was. After personal bequests, he wished the bulk of his estate to be used for devising a new English alphabet. Forseeing, however, that there might be problems attached to this—and there were—he made provision for an alternative: that his money should be distributed between the British Museum, where he first learned of Socialism, the National Gallery of Ireland, where he got his first taste of the value and beauty of artistic creation, and the Royal Academy of Dramatic Art, as a pledge to the future of his own art form, drama.

A note on the play: performance and publication

The writing of *The Devil's Disciple* began in 1896 and the play was completed in 1897. The copyright performance—a necessity before international author's copyright came into force legally—took place in 1897, as did its first American performance, Shaw's first commercial success. The first British production was given at the Princess of Wales Theatre, Kennington, on 26 September 1899. A critique in the influential newspaper, *The Times*, was favourable neither to the production nor to the play. Of the production, the critic noted: 'There were times when the assistance of a prompter was required—and times, too, when the assistance appeared not be forthcoming.' Of the play itself, he wrote: '*The Devil's Disciple* is full of that mordant satire with which we are familiar in Mr Shaw's work and full, too, of that sense of insincerity, of mere posing which mars so much of it . . . . At the most thrilling moments in his plays he will throw his situation to the winds in order to poke sly fun at his characters or his public . . . . He sets out, apparently, with the intention of writing a drama of emotion, of sentiment even. For an act or two this mood lasts. Then he tires of his puppets, and finishes the play in a mood that is frankly whimsical and absurd.' If Shaw expressed strong opinions of his own, his writings certainly attracted strong opinions from others.

The play first appeared in a collection entitled *Three Plays for Puritans* in 1901. The volume, which contained, apart from *The Devil's Disciple*, *Caesar and Cleopatra*, *Captain Brassbound's Conversion* and an extensive preface, was published by Grant Richards, London, in an edition of 2,500 copies. A Limited Collected Edition of Shaw's plays was started by Constable, London, under his personal supervision, in 1930, and in 1931 the Standard Edition of his works, including much of his music and drama criticism, began to appear, again under the Constable imprint. The *Complete Plays* were issued by Constable, London, in 1931, and the *Complete Prefaces* by the same publisher in 1934. Enlarged versions of both volumes together with new prefaces by Shaw were published later in a cheaper edition by Odhams, London, and in July 1946, in celebration of Shaw's ninetieth birthday, Penguin Books, Harmondsworth, published a ten-volume set of his works.

Shaw was at great pains to ensure that his published work was as accurate as was possible, and he corrected proofs meticulously. In an interview given in 1928 about his latest work, *The Intelligent Woman's Guide to Socialism and Capitalism* (1928), Shaw said:

> About my new book there is one thing about which I am very proud. It is the care I have taken to eliminate as many blank spaces as possible, caused by short lines in the letterpress. You know that a true craftsman is proud of his work and wants it to be as perfect as possible. You would not credit the time I have put into reading and altering the proofs of this book to get the spacing just right.

The plays of George Bernard Shaw are, then, published as the author intended them to be played, with all the information about the characters and with all the stage directions that he felt were necessary to an accurate presentation of his ideas, his characters and his dialogue.

Part 2

Summaries
of THE DEVIL'S DISCIPLE

A general summary

The Devil's Disciple is a play about finding a man's true destiny
through testing his ability to decide and act. Two questions are posed
by the play: (*a*) how may a man be true to his own spiritually vital
nature in a spiritually dead society; (*b*) when independence is threatened by oppression what obligations has a man of spirit towards his
fellow men. The oppressors in the play are rigid Puritanism and the
colonial power of the British troops. The dramatic judgement on the
validity of a character's ultimate destiny is based on his response to
these two questions.

The action follows the fortunes of Richard Dudgeon. Returning
home to hear the last will and testament of his father, Richard offends
his puritanical relatives by proclaiming his allegiance to the devil. His
seemingly irreligious behaviour particularly shocks Judith Anderson,
the beautiful young wife of the local minister, Anthony Anderson.
Later that day, in Anderson's house, Judith's assessment of Richard is
radically altered. He bravely takes the place of her husband when
British troops come to arrest the man of God. Stunned by Richard's
generous spirit as much as by his farewell kiss, Judith interprets her
husband's decision to leave the town immediately and quickly only as
an act of cowardice. During Richard's brief imprisonment and trial she
holds to her vision of him as a true and noble man, although he rejects
her emotionalism and only allows her to attend the trial on condition
that she will not betray his identity. Richard's vigorous and treasonable
statements at his trial ensure that even when his identity becomes
known he is still condemned to death by hanging. The timely entry of
Anthony Anderson, who has forsaken his ministry for a captaincy in
the militia and is protected by a safe-conduct pass, halts the execution.
Judith, attracted back to Anderson by his new character, begs Richard
to keep the secret of her faltering affection. When the play ends the
man of God has found his true destiny as a man of action, and the erst-
while man of action, Richard Dudgeon, has found his true destiny as a
spiritual Puritan. By rebelling against his oppressors each man can find
his own true nature and fulfil his social and his spiritual obligations.

Detailed summaries

Act I

Although one of their number was executed that day, all is quiet in the Dudgeon household until Mrs Dudgeon, asleep by the fire, is rudely awakened by her son, Christy, who brings news of her husband's sudden death. Her reaction is one of annoyance rather than grief, and it is with mounting anger that she hears from the minister, Anthony Anderson, that her reprobate son, Richard, is returning to the house to hear the reading of his father's will. When Richard enters he brings a breath of life and vigour into the dismal room. His wit and energy, his ready sympathy for his illegitimate cousin, Essie, impress more than the unchristian and uncaring attitudes of the religious Mrs Dudgeon and her family. Richard's main purpose is to shock the gathering and in this he succeeds, especially horrifying Judith, Anderson's young and pretty wife; she, in particular, is outraged by his irreligious stance. To the consternation of the assembled family, the will ensures that Richard inherits all the property. He vows freedom and protection for the weak in the house where he is master, and jokingly warns his relatives and the minister of the likelihood of an execution since British troops are advancing on the town and will require the exemplary hanging of a rebel.

Act I forms the exposition of the play. In it the audience are introduced to the main characters, to the historical background, to the beginnings of the plot, to the style and to the themes. The central characters of Richard Dudgeon and Judith and Anthony Anderson are quickly established and the triangular relationship which is to develop in Act II is hinted at by Judith's strong physical reaction to Richard and by Anderson's tolerance of his irreligious posture. The subsidiary characters establish the historical background to the main figures: the American War of Independence (1776–83) is shown as coming close to this isolated town by the forward march of British troops with their constant threat of execution; the repressive puritanical sects of New England who hold dominance in this town and in this house are sharply delineated in the figure of Mrs Dudgeon. The beginnings of the plot are seen in the independent stand of Richard Dudgeon who in this act is opposed to his family's oppressive puritanism and who in Act II will be opposed to political oppression by the colonial power. The tension between the use of religious and military language and imagery which characterises the play's puritans is seen in the speeches of Richard, Anderson and Mrs Dudgeon, and Shaw's tendency towards the use of balanced epigrammatic patterning, which he brings to its high point in the language of Burgoyne, is also present. Finally, the themes of the play—the search for destiny, the need for a vital determining life force, the need to distinguish inner reality from outward form—are suggested by the contradictory descriptions of Anderson's character, by Richard's contradictory behaviour but consistent, sharply intelligent reactions, and by the self-betrayal of Mrs Dudgeon's unchristian Christianity.

NOTES AND GLOSSARY:

1777: the year 1777 marked the turning point of the American War of Independence. The plan of campaign by Sir John Burgoyne (1723–92) and Sir William Howe (1729–1814), the senior British generals in America, was a failure largely because of poor communications; meanwhile the colonists, the rebels, increased in strength

New Hampshire: one of the districts (now States), in New England on the eastern coast of the United States of America

Websterbridge: a fictitious town. Later evidence in the play suggests a proximity to Saratoga, scene of the defeat of General Burgoyne by the rebel American forces

prepossessing: making a favourable impression

matron: a married woman or an elderly woman of sober habits

dominion: rule over subordinates

felony: crime

seventh commandment: 'Thou shalt not steal' was the seventh commandment given by God to Moses

missed a Sunday: missed a Sunday religious service

Rights of Man: in general, the rights, now enshrined in the American constitution, of every citizen to 'life, liberty and the pursuit of happiness'. Specifically, *The Rights of Man* (1791–2) was a highly influential book by the revolutionary writer Thomas Paine (1737–1809)

fender of iron laths: a fire guard made from straight pieces of iron

hobs and boiler: the surfaces beside a fire where food could be kept warm and the part of the fire used for boiling

tin sconce: tin candlestick with a handle

iron weights: the mechanism of some clocks was regulated by the motion of two large weights

dresser: a kitchen sideboard on which crockery could be displayed

hardly cold in his grave: recently dead

I dropped off: I fell asleep

after me waiting: when I have waited. This is one of a number of Irish idioms which appear at the beginning of the play

mend the fire: bring the fire back to life. Another specifically Irish idiom

plaid: a woollen cloth usually patterned in tartan

the devil's work: sin is regarded as the work of the devil. In this case, Mrs Dudgeon feels justified in calling Essie a bastard because her illegitimate birth was the result of sin

like a stuck pig: like a pig stabbed by a stick. A 'sticker' is a person who kills pigs

as a rebel: as an American rebel against the lawful British government

plucks her shawl... over her ears: a traditional gesture of mourning. Notice, however, that Mrs Dudgeon makes the gesture 'vexedly', in annoyance rather than grief

It's sinful: Mrs Dudgeon feels that her husband's lack of responsibility shown by his inconvenient death can be regarded as a sin

the scum of the earth: worthless people. The phrase was first used about an army. The Duke of Wellington said his own British army was 'composed of the scum of the earth'

Sister: a Puritan form of address. In a community all members were regarded as brothers and sisters

The Lord has laid his hand very heavily upon you: God has given you a great distress to bear. Note the biblical quality of this and later passages

I must bear my cross: I must endure this painful experience. This is a pious comparison to Christ's stoical endurance of Calvary

least said is soonest mended: a proverb. Difficulties can be overcome more easily if they are not talked about at length

Wasnt it only natural: wasn't it according to the laws of nature

prodigal son: in Scripture, the prodigal son wastes his inheritance but is nevertheless welcomed home by his father. See the Bible, Luke 15:11–32

We are told that the wicked shall be punished: 'as wax melteth before the fire, so let the wicked perish at the presence of God'. See the Bible, Psalms 68:2

their Maker's word: the laws of God

his heavenly judge: God

softheaded: stupid

new will: a will or testament can be altered by the testator at any time as long as he is of sound mind and the document is witnessed

marriage portion: dowry, the money a woman brings to her marriage

the heart of man is deceitful in all things: a quotation from the Bible, Jeremiah 17:9; 'The heart is deceitful above all things, and desperately wicked'

you are not worthy to loose his shoe latchet: you are unworthy to perform even a menial task for him. A scriptural reference to the Gospel of St John where John the Baptist deplores his own unworthiness before Christ 'Whose shoe's latchet I am not worthy to unloose'. See John 1:27

Godfearing man: a man who reverences God

followed your heart in your marriage: married for love rather than for duty. Note how the heart is a negative mode of judgement for Mrs Dudgeon but a positive one for Anthony Anderson

His law: the law of God

Get up out of that: get up and stop this laziness (an Irish idiom)

toasting yourself: warming yourself by the fire

barnbrack: a bread containing dried fruit

ink-stand: container for ink and pens

keep a civil tongue in your head: be polite, courteous

stopping here: remaining here

bonnet: a woman's hat tied on by strings or ribbons

too religious: too conscious of their own spiritual worth

plays games on Sunday: to engage in such activities on the Sabbath was to break the third commandment: 'Thou shalt keep holy the Sabbath day'

gaiters: covering for the ankles which fitted down over the shoe

We are all equal before the Throne: at God's final judgement on our lives we will all be considered as equals. The Throne is the throne of God, the seat of His majesty in heaven

republican sentiment: equality of status was one of the primary objectives in the American and French revolutions. In the original draft of the American Declaration of Independence Thomas Jefferson (1743–1829), who was later to become President of the United States, wrote: 'We hold these truths to be sacred and undeniable; that all men are created equal and independent, that from that equal creation they derive rights inherent and inalienable, among which are the preservation of life, and liberty, and the pursuit of happiness'. A hierarchical society ruled by those who considered themselves superior would be distasteful to all true republicans. Here the term is transferred to religion: the women feel that they are members of the Puritan Elect and therefore superior to the illegitimate Essie

the eyes of a fanatic: the eyes of one who has a strong purpose in life. Shaw would suggest that Richard is a religious fanatic, zealous in the pursuit of his own spiritual cause

your very humble servant: a polite form of address used ironically by Richard so as to make it 'a comprehensive insult'

a negligent wicket keeper: a player of the game of cricket who has not kept his concentration on the game

keeping up appearances: attending to outward appearances so as to conceal inner realities

upright: of righteous character. Here it is ironically juxtaposed with the term 'horsedealer' which implies 'cheat'

come forth: an ironic use of the scriptural phrase. Jesus commanded the dead Lazarus to come forth from his tomb (see John 11:43). Notice the number of times that Richard uses quotations from the Bible which he bends to his own use

shepherding: looking after sheep. The term 'shepherd', following scriptural usage, is frequently applied to a minister of religion

clink a glass: have a drink

Pastor: Minister, priest

unction: religious glibness

company sherry: a sweet, mildly alcoholic drink, reserved in this household for times when visitors were present

a temperate man: a man who does not drink alcohol

a good woman: a woman given to good works. This would normally be considered a compliment but Richard sees Judith's puritanical goodness as an offence against *his* religion

irregular child: illegitimate child

checkmated: trapped by an opponent's move. The reference is to a move in the game of chess where defensive movement is effectively stopped by an opponent's skill *railed chair*:   a chair whose back is made of a series of wooden struts shaped like the structure of a ladder

damned: condemned to Hell for his evil deeds

hope in the eyes of a child: a child is a common Romantic symbol of innocence and purity. Shaw has been at pains to establish Essie as the Rousseau-like child of natural feeling and behaviour in this unnatural religious household. See Shaw's description of Essie at the beginning of the play

proper legal phraseology: there is a correct form of words to be used in the making of a will. However, a will is still legal even if the legal form of words has not been used

without the consolation of the law: an ironic turn of the usual phrase: 'without the consolations of religion'

For what . . . thankful: ironic usage of the grace or prayer normally used before eating a meal

of sound mind: sane. It is a legal requirement that the testator should have full and complete knowledge of the distribution of his property

I recommend . . . children: I ask my children to look after her for her goodness and piety and forgive her for them. Here again, as in Richard's speeches, goodness and piety are seen as negative, repressive forces

the word I gave to it: robbery

The fatted calf: another reference to the biblical parable of the prodigal son. When the son returned home having wasted all his heritage his father killed the fatted calf, a most valuable animal, to serve it at the thanksgiving feast. See Luke 15:23

live in clover: literally, live in fields full of clover, a plant which horses love; metaphorically, live in a state of pleasurable luxury

the best room: a room in a farmhouse not used by the family but kept for entertaining visitors

into my Maker's hands: into the care of my God

Amen: a word commonly used at the end of a prayer. It means 'so be it' and Mrs Dudgeon cannot say 'so be it' to this will which deprives her of her rights

the courts will sustain . . . woman: under the law of *primogeniture* the eldest son inherits the family property. At that time, 1777, women had no property rights. Consequently, if a man wished to disinherit his wife he could do so quite legally and the courts would sustain his will

cock of the walk: the most important person here. The metaphor is taken from the behaviour of cocks and hens in a farmyard; the cock 'rules the roost'

proofs of the greatness...insignificance: Mrs Dudgeon accepts this calamity as proof of the power of God and of her own importance

Mary Wollstonecraft: Mary Wollstonecraft (1759–97) was the author of one of the first books which advocated political, social and economic rights for women, *A Vindication of the Rights of Women* (1790). She was married to the philosopher William Godwin (1756–1836) who influenced many of the political radicals of the time, among them Paine, Blake and, later, the poet P.B. Shelley (1792–1822) who married Mary Wollstonecraft's daughter

a good girl: once again Richard's questions are double-edged. In his vocabulary 'good' is a negative term; in the vocabulary of the others, it is a positive term

the devil: the spirit of evil. In Christian mythology the devil was cast out of heaven because, in his pride, he would not serve God. *Non serviam* (Latin), 'I will not serve', is the motto of the devil. In William Blake's (1757–1827) poem, *The Marriage of Heaven and Hell* (1791), the devil is seen as a force of positive energy. It is in this sense that Richard uses the term, though, of course, the others interpret it according to orthodox teaching

sermons: pious exhortations given by a preacher. The balance of this sentence gives the audience the first clear indication of the relationship between Richard and Anthony: Richard, too, despite appearances, is a 'preacher' and 'a religious man'

the Devil's Disciple: the follower of the devil and one who believes in his teaching. The term 'disciple' is usually used of the followers of Christ who not only accepted his teaching but sought to bring it to others. Disciples, in other words, had a religious mission similar to that of a preacher

I was brought up....man of me: this speech is typical of the dual vocabularies of Richard Dudgeon and Anthony Anderson. Both men draw their speeches from religious and military terminologies. This underlines the changing fortunes of both during the course of the play, where the man of action

becomes the man of words and *vice versa*.
'Service', 'natural master', 'captain', 'the right',
'conqueror', 'swore an oath', are all terms taken
from a military background: Dick has enlisted in
the army of the devil

I promised him my soul: selling one's soul to the devil was usually
based on a bargain: the half-mythical Dr Faustus
(fl. 1507–40), for example, sold his in return for
some years of youth. Richard, however, *freely*
promises his soul. His is an individual choice,
made by his own will

martial law: rule by military forces. This is the audience's first
indication of the imminent approach of the
soldiers

gallows: a wooden frame used for hanging criminals

King George: George III (1738–1820), the reigning English
monarch, who refused to accept the demands of
the colonists

up hill and down dale: all over the land

have conducted the service: a service of prayer for the defeat of the
British forces. Apart from Shaw's initial
description of Anderson's appearance, this is our
first indication of Anderson's sympathy with the
rebels

your family bible: the prized possession of many households, usually
containing a record of the names of the family for
generations

a brace of pistols: a pair of hand-guns. As in his appearance, his
unlikely marriage, his inability to comfort his
parishioners, here once again Anderson is seen as
not conforming to the orthodox view of a Christian minister. And once again the religious and
military vocabularies are opposed; 'family bible'
and 'brace of pistols'

dancing on nothing: suspended from the gallows a hanged man in his
death agonies will involuntarily jerk his legs. This
is referred to as 'dancing on the end of a rope' or
'dancing on nothing'

meant business: was serious in his intent. Since the Devil's Disciple
was regarded by all as an evil person his execution
would prove nothing. The execution of pillars of
the community, however, would act as a salutary
example to others and lessen the likelihood of
rebellion

run up the American flag: hoist the flag of rebellion

fight for freedom: fight for political freedom. Richard also wants to fight for individual freedom and it is Anderson who takes over the fight for political freedom

My dying curse: a stock gesture of melodrama. A mother's curse was traditionally meant to be very powerful, bringing dreadful misfortune on the offending child. Coming from such a mother as Mrs Dudgeon, however, the curse is interpreted by Richard as a form of blessing

baptism: the Christian naming and first blessing of a child by symbolically pouring water on its head. The ceremony cleanses and purifies the recipient as Richard is here purified by the Romantic symbol of the tears of a child

Act II

The living room of the Anderson household is more homely and comforting than the dreary austerity of the Dudgeon home. On returning to this welcoming room, Anthony Anderson tells his wife that he has invited Richard Dudgeon to their home in order to apprise him of the danger he may be in from the advancing troops. Although Richard had previously announced that a minister like Anderson was a much more likely candidate for hanging than a reprobate like himself, Anderson still feels that it is his duty to warn Richard to avoid the troops. Judith remains uncomfortable in Richard's presence but agrees to take tea alone with him when Anderson has to go out unexpectedly to attend the dying Mrs Dudgeon. This domestic scene is rudely interrupted by the arrival of the troops intent on arresting Anderson. When, mistaking Richard for Anderson, they arrest the Devil's Disciple, Richard persuades Judith to keep his secret and protect her husband. She is overwhelmed by his bravery and his farewell kiss causes her to faint. Sometime later her husband returns and further misunderstandings occur when Judith, trapped by her promise of secrecy, tries to prevent him from going to see Richard at the barracks. When Anderson finds out that Richard has been arrested in mistake for him, he rushes from the house taking only his coat, his guns and money and leaving Judith under the mistaken impression that he is running away from danger.

The second act builds on the exposition of the first. The three central characters are thrown into sharp relief in this act and both Richard and Anderson make their decisions: Richard, following his independent spirit, to sacrifice himself for his fellow man; Anderson to exchange his ministry for his brace of pistols. Judith is revealed in her true character: reacting emotionally rather than logically, she is egocentric and superficial in her judgements. The religious conflict of the play is interrupted by the intrusion of political conflict represented by the soldiers, and the historical background of Act I gains prominence in the action of Act II. This act, therefore, clarifies the two catalysts of action in this play, the two agents which initiate every significant action: religion and politics. Both Richard Dudgeon and Anthony Anderson are faced with a decision which has to combine religious and political principles. The emphasis of their decisions is, however, unexpected: the minister acts, as we discover later, largely from political motives whereas Richard is motivated by a vague spiritual principle based on the truth of his own nature.

NOTES AND GLOSSARY:

griddle: a flat iron plate for baking bread and cakes

hob: a surface near the fire used for keeping food hot

fingerplates: plates to protect doors from dirty fingers

treacle: dark brown sugar syrup

japanned: varnished in the Japanese style

trencher: a large plate or platter

crock: earthenware dish

social pretensions: wish to show herself of higher social standing than she was

drugget: a coarsely woven woollen rug

mezzotint: a picture from a copperplate etching which has blurred rather than sharp lines

copperplate: a sharply delineated etching

rococo: of elaborate ornamental design. The high rococo period of art occurred during the seventeenth and eighteenth centuries. Late nineteenth century design favoured a return to functional domestic architecture

Philip Webb: Philip Webb (1851–1915) was an architect and designer. Webb's designs predominantly followed the theories of William Morris (1834–96)

The town clock is always fast: this is a piece of information which is later of vital importance in delaying Richard's execution

A bugle call: the call of an army bugle. The presence of the soldiers, who were six miles away at the end of the last act, is thus established as a near and real threat

King George: (the forces of) King George

Soldiers don't . . . town: the operations of soldiers are not subtle, they act directly and noisily, not bothering about the forms. This is the way that Anderson will later behave, not bothering to equivocate as does Richard

in this world . . . afraid of it: the words of a man who does not himself know fear

He said what he thought . . . frighten me: Anderson sees through the gestures of Dick Dudgeon and perceives a touch of the actor in his pose

blasphemer: a person who insults God. Judith feels she would be justified in hating such a man

to be indifferent: not to care. Anderson, and Shaw, considered love or hate to be strong emotions, and found any show of strength preferable to inhuman indifference

how like hate is to love: any strong emotion is capable of turning into its opposite. The audience has already seen Judith's strong physical reaction to Richard in Act I

tax one another: put unbearable burdens on one another

fonder of Richard . . . me: Anderson with his clear-sighted intuition has observed the powerful response of Judith to the 'man of action', Richard

caddy: container for tea-leaves

stands on much ceremony: is over-careful about their social behaviour

Raining like the very: the sentence is left unfinished. Richard is presumably about to use some word which would be offensive to a lady

The magic of property: the attraction of a wealthy person. Richard implies that the minister's attitude towards him has changed because he is now a wealthy man

to preach: to give a sermon

I am no great preacher: I am not talented at preaching. Since preaching is one of the major requirements of a minister, the audience is here given one more indication of Anderson's unsuitability for his calling

a free man: one not bound by duty or vocation

so pressing: so eager in her invitations

break bread: partake of your meal. Scriptural echoes of Christ's Last Supper make the breaking of bread a gesture of trust and faith

to draw: to infuse, for the tea-leaves to impart their flavour to the water

a great enemy: like 'devil' and 'good', the term 'enemy' is used in two senses. Both Richard and Anthony Anderson use the term to mean 'possessor of a violently opposed energy but one who can be respected'. Under this definition, such forces of energy can easily turn to friendship or love

turn a compliment: say something flattering by altering the terms of reference

contrariness: perverse desire to hold contradictory opinions

I am ... what I am: In apologising for his own unworthiness, Richard echoes the words of God to Moses in the Bible: 'I AM THAT I AM' (Exodus 3:14)

it's almost holy: the peace and domesticity of the minister's house have a spiritual quality which Richard recognises

duty: this is one of the key words of the play. Here it is the sergeant who must do his duty, but Mrs Dudgeon, Anderson, Judith, Burgoyne and Richard all follow the dictates of what they see as their duty

steadfast in my religion: an unswerving disciple of the devil's religion

Youre a game one: you're a brave man. The sergeant speaks in a cockney dialect rendered phonetically by Shaw. He was later to exploit this accent to great effect in the character of Eliza Doolittle in *Pygmalion*

to bin a soldier: to have been a soldier

them two: those two (soldiers)

Muffle the drums: drums were traditionally muffled for the dead march

you may as well dream a cup of tea: the practical good humour of Anderson is in sharp contrast to the heroic, idealistic gestures of Richard

to know that I had run ... danger: the metaphor is taken from a military vocabulary. Anderson who has sold the family bible for a brace of pistols sees it as his duty to be alert and at his post

my duty: Judith is trapped by conflicting duties: (a) she must save her husband; (b) she must save the man who has helped her husband. The two are irreconcilable

I know you will take .... no power: Judith is caught between two strong men who follow their own decisions. Essentially she is a pawn between them and they dispose of her casually at the end of the play. She is quite irrelevant to their main concerns

For me!!!:   up to this point much of the tension of the scene has derived from the minister's ignorance of the true situation and the audience's awareness of it. It is with his sudden realisation of the truth that the audience witness the change of Anthony Anderson from the 'man of peace' to a 'formidable man of war' filled with 'brute energy''

Blood an' owns!:   blood and wounds. A blasphemous oath, swearing by Christ's blood and wounds. It is an exclamation more suited to a soldier than a minister

You are deserting him: Judith has already been established as a woman of limited imagination; she misunderstands the natures of both men

Hold your tongue: be quiet

powder horn: a flask for carrying gunpowder

Can we pray . . . neck?: he realises the impracticality of prayer where direct physical action is required

I am not God: the careless and flippant use of the name of God was regarded as blasphemous and was, of course, doubly shocking coming from the mouth of a so-called man of God

Minister be: Minister be (damned)

Now listen, you: the command is more like that of a soldier to a subordinate than of a loving husband to his wife

you may depend on him to the death: a romantic gesture of little practical use and as such receives an appropriate, if harsh, reply from Anderson

You dont know the man youre married to: Judith thought she had married Pastor Anderson whereas she is now the wife of Captain Anderson

And waste another half minute: Anderson's practical impatience may by compared with Dick's more romantic leave-taking

He has gone to save himself: Judith misunderstands the speed and urgency of her husband's departure

---

Act III

Judith visits Richard in prison and begs him to save himself by disclosing his true identity. Richard, however, rejects her pleas saying that solidarity of man with man is necessary in the cause of independence. When she declares her love for him and insinuates that she thinks he performed his heroic action for her benefit, he turns from her in scorn claiming that he is not motivated by love but rather by his own nature which refused to allow him to buy his life at the expense of another. At his insistence, she vows to keep his secret and to remain quiet at his trial.

The trial introduces the audience to General Burgoyne and Major Swindon, the latter a stereotype soldier, the former an urbane, sophisticated figure who has little taste for the task he is about to undertake. From their conversation it is apparent that the rebellion has met with some success and that the British position of military superiority is under threat. Burgoyne's wit and Richard's response to it enliven the trial where the Devil's Disciple makes several treasonable statements thereby ensuring his own execution. Judith, who deplores the levity of the whole proceedings, can no longer tolerate the thought of Richard's death and betrays his identity. Nevertheless, although his real identity is confirmed by Christy Dudgeon, the due process of military law cannot be stopped and Richard is condemned to death. After Richard is led away, Burgoyne confides in Swindon that the rebels are sending a captain of militia under a safe-conduct pass to negotiate with them. He further confesses that due to a bureaucratic error his proposed joint campaign with another British general is impossible and he is left in a position of almost certain defeat.

The execution of Richard Dudgeon is prepared with great pomp and ceremony. Richard rejects the traditional comfort of a clergyman, pre-ferring to remain true to his own religion. As the execution is about to begin Anthony Anderson rushes in. He announces his identity but produces a safe-conduct pass which shows him to be Captain Anderson of the militia. In this hour of his country's need he has found his true destiny and predicts that Richard will find his—as a true religious man. The play closes with the sounds of a British march fading in the distance, overcome by the triumphal American rebel song, 'Yankee Doodle Dandy'.

Act III brings the action of the play to its conclusion. The main characters have developed through their respective trials and have come to accept their true destinies. Both Richard and Anderson have been forced to declare their true colours and Judith has become merely an irrelevance to both; the idealists have no real need of her ineffectual emotionalism. Religious and political conflict become one as Richard quotes Scripture back at his captors, showing them that an ostentatious religious presence does not excuse murder. The introduction of the character of Burgoyne provides an interesting balance for Richard and Anderson. He, too, is a superior man as is shown by his wit, his humour and his decisiveness. His robust acceptance of the limitations imposed by the conditions of his army on the execution of his duty provides a foil to the absolutist nature of the decisions of the other main characters.

NOTES AND GLOSSARY:

mum: madam
kep: kept
Bridewell: gaol, a place of imprisonment
court martial: a court held by officers of a military force for offences against the laws of the service. In times of war civilians, too, are sometimes tried by courts martial
slep: slept
made a rare good breakfast: ate an unusually large breakfast
spoil five: a card game drawn, or spoiled, if no player wins three out of five tricks
tramp: sound of marching feet
General Burgoyne: General Sir John Burgoyne was a historical figure who played a major part in the campaign of 1777. Burgoyne was to march down from Canada and join forces with Howe marching up from New York. However, because of bureaucratic incompetence, Howe never began his campaign and Burgoyne, already far into enemy territory was heavily defeated on 17 October at the battle of Saratoga. Shaw's basic delineation of Burgoyne's character was derived from the account of his life in Edward de Fonblanque's *Political and Military Episodes in the Latter Half of the Eighteenth Century* (1876)
served with him in Portugal: was among the troops under his command in a military campaign in Portugal
count on: be sure you will have
by your leave: with your permission
on the wing: flown, gone away
He is no longer my husband: Judith's rejection of her husband and his supposed cowardice at the end of Act II is reinforced here. It establishes her essential triviality and lack of trust. Shaun, in the Irish dramatist Dion Boucicault's (1822–90) melodrama *Arrah-Na-Pogue* (1864), suggests to Fanny, a similar character to Judith, that she 'did not love him (Beamish, her lover and his lord) well enough to trust him'. Judith Anderson shows a similar lack of faith
What good would his staying do?: Richard echoes the practicality of Anderson's attitude in the previous act

I can find no manner of reason for acting as I did: it is one of the weak-est points of the plot that Richard acts without any clear motivation. Shaw attempted to defend Richard's instinctive decision saying that such deeds happen every day. However, the dramatic effect is ultimately a bit unconvincing

at my door: my responsibility

to cow us: to subjugate us, to make us fearful

That is the only force ... nation: national and personal soldiering is the most potent force in achieving nationhood and ridding the country of the forces of oppression

across the Atlantic: from America to Britain

what does all that matter?: such political considerations as national independence are meaningless to Judith

men have ... strange notions: Shaw is simultaneously poking fun at the conventional 'masculine' aspirations towards heroism and Judith's inability even to appreciate their existence

And I!: Judith's reaction to Richard's probable death is similar to that of Mrs Dudgeon on being told of her husband's death. Both women are egocentric, car-ing more for their own feelings than for the sensibilities of others. Judith is an unusual woman among Shaw's female characters, most of whom are independent, strong and intelligent. She, how-ever, is a more typically melodramatic heroine: pretty, weak, swayed by emotion and placed in a situation where she is tested beyond her capacity.

divining: intuitively seeing

presently: soon

like a dog: unwanted dogs were often disposed of by hanging

in love: swayed by their hearts rather than their heads. As a true Puritan Richard treats such a reaction with scorn. Compare his response to Anthony Ander-son's insistence on the heart as the organ of true judgement in Act I

the law of my own nature: the force that makes me what I am, my inner spirit which forces me to obey its laws

gallows or no gallows: whether or not I was to be hanged

with fierce contempt: Richard does not understand that an action could be motivated by feelings of love and is contemptuous of anyone who feels it could

keep faith: keep to your promises

canopy: a covering hung over a throne

monogram: personal initials. In this case, they are G.R., the
                       abbreviation for (Latin) *Georgius Rex*, King
                       George
maroon: deep crimson
by an elopement: by running away to get married
poor devil: a conventional phrase which gains ironic effect
                       here since the 'minister' is the Devil's Disciple
Martyrdom: death in the service of a cause or an ideal which is
                       generally religious in its origins
Martyrdom ... is what these people like: a rebellion or a revolution is
                       frequently encouraged rather than discouraged by
                       the execution of a number of its soldiers: these
                       become symbols and rallying points against the
                       enemy
We have arranged .... try him: the customary legal order has been
                       reversed: the punishment has been arranged before
                       the trial has taken place
I do not express my opinion: the proper soldier deals in facts not
                       opinions
profane language: language offensive to holy things. In Burgoyne's
                       vocabulary facts are sacred, opinions profane
your supports: your system of scouts in the surrounding neigh-
                       bourhood
in the hands of: under the control of
the British soldier will give a good account of himself: the British
                       soldier will do his duty well. Major Swindon con-
                       sistently speaks in jingoistic clichés, in convention-
                       al phrases which show an uncritical, indeed an
                       unthinking patriotism. He is a military machine
                       whose duty it is to respond to orders
And therefore ... business: Shaw was critical of the type of stupid
                       heroic action in which many ordinary men died
                       because of lack of thought on the part of the
                       officers. Burgoyne, witty, intelligent and practical,
                       is Shaw's mouthpiece in the play. He is 'a superior
                       man', his mind is unclouded by the idealisms of
                       Anthony Anderson and Richard Dudgeon, and his
                       judgements, while practical, are urbane and
                       sympathetic
pretend to: aspire to, hope to have
the devotion of my countrymen: another melodramatic cliché
writing a melodrama: patriotic melodramas in which characters
                       voiced such sentiments were popular at the time. It
                       is also, of course, a theatrical metaphor which

deepens the illusion of action: characters in a melo-drama talking about characters in a melodrama

bluff: a hearty show of self-confidence, covering a weakness

sheepishness: stupidity, unwillingness to act on one's own initiative

Hessians, Brunswickers, German dragoons: German soldiers. The 'English' occupation force in America was largely composed of German troops in the service of George III, himself a member of the German royal house of Hanover. It is therefore unreal as well as impractical for Swindon to speak of the 'devotion of [his] countrymen'

Suppose the colonists find a leader: given their numerical superiority, if the colonists found a strong leader they could easily overcome the occupation forces. This is the first hint to the audience of where Anthony Anderson might have gone

Our duty: Major Swindon adds another 'duty' to the conflict of duties in the play

thrown a flood of light: illuminated, made clear. It is a theatrical metaphor for using a particular type of lamp which lights a large area of the stage

dissenter: one who dissents. The term is generally used of those who belonged to religious sects not part of the Established Church, the Church of England

sit at the feet of Gamaliel: sit at the feet of a learned man. The phrase is used ironically here. It was St Paul who learned the law 'at the feet of Gamaliel'. See the Bible, Acts 22:3

trying circumstances: difficult circumstances

I stand rebuked: I acknowledge you were just to correct me. The remark is heavily ironic, Burgoyne has intentionally misunderstood Swindon's use of 'your'

I am an American: this statement is treasonable, implying as it does, the rejection of British citizenship

I may as well be hanged for a sheep as a lamb: well-known saying which means that if a man is to be executed for committing a small crime he might as well commit a bigger crime and be executed for that instead

a gentleman: a man who was well educated and knew how to behave in society

political necessity ... ill-feeling: the clear intellectual power of Burgoyne sees no necessity to feel ill-will towards his opponent. What has to be done is done out of necessity and duty, not out of spite or bad feeling

I object to Lord North's robbing me: Frederick, Lord North (1732–92), who became the British Prime Minister in 1770, was largely responsible for the measures which brought about the loss of the American colonies: punitive taxation and unfair restrictions on trade

pig-headed lunatic: George III was very fat and was frequently caricatured as a pig. He also suffered from periodic fits of insanity which became worse as he aged. Eventually, the monarchy was entrusted to the Prince Regent, who later reigned briefly as George IV

does not allow of: does not permit. Like a good soldier, Burgoyne does not express his political views in public. The audience is, however, given to understand that Burgoyne is not a great supporter of the monarch

An unusual taste: hanging is an unusual thing for anybody to desire

the streets barricaded: blockages across the streets which would have prevented the army entering them

house loopholed: houses provided with apertures through which snipers could fire

in arms: ready to fight

a prisoner of war: a prisoner of war is, by definition, a soldier and as such entitled to be shot rather than hanged. Hanging is a civilian punishment

marksmanship: skill in shooting at a target

a firing party: a group of soldiers commanded to execute a prisoner by shooting him

the provo-marshall's pistol: the provost-marshal in charge of a firing squad had the duty to 'finish off' the execution if the soldiers had failed to kill their victim

I have told ... ten times over: Richard, during the course of the trial, has made so many treasonable statements that the court would condemn him whatever his identity. Disclosing it now, therefore, will serve no useful purpose

a black cap and so forth: traditionally the English judge put on a black cap to pronounce the sentence of death on a prisoner

in a red coat: in the uniform of a British soldier

that you are not his wife: that you are his mistress, living with him but not legally married to him

We are bound to: we have to, we are obliged to

independent testimony: the statement of a witness who is not personally involved

Dispatches: military reports

Dead beat with: exhausted from

too well brought up...in him: repressive upbringing under the puritanical Mrs Dudgeon has taken away from Christy sense—ability to decide and act intelligently—and manhood—a realisation of selfhood and an ability to live his life in accordance with his own belief

jumping jackass: donkey, stupid person, idiot

zany: idiot

blithering baboon: stupid ape, idiot

understrapper: subordinate

raise the devil in me: make me angry

oatmeal: a pale grey-coloured grain

a safe-conduct: a pass which would guarantee the bearer that he would not be harmed

their militia: the armed force of the rebels

mob of rebellious tradesmen: an undisciplined and inexperienced force

I will undertake...united forces: this was the actual plan of campaign for the troops under Howe and Burgoyne. A pincer movement was designed to trap the rebel forces. Unfortunately for Burgoyne, Howe remained in New York and Burgoyne's forces were defeated at the Battle of Saratoga

Jobbery: political corruption by bribery

Red Tape: excessive attention to the processes of bureaucracy, so called from the red tape with which bundles of official papers were tied

disobeyed orders: a failure to obey orders is incomprehensible to the professional soldier Swindon

pillory: a wooden frame supported by a post with holes through which a criminal's head and hands were put as a punishment

whipping post: a post to which a criminal would be tied to be whipped as a punishment

stocks: similar to a pillory but also containing holes for a criminal's legs

the town beadle: an official of the town with the power to punish petty offenders

fixed bayonets: rifles to which bayonets or stabbing knives have been attached

Dress: a military order to come into line formation
Out of it: get out of the way
Some o: some of
strung up: hanged
Hoosians: Hessians, German soldiers
talk to their toes . . . muskets: hit them on their toes with the wooden end of a gun
no call here: no business to be here
argufying: arguing
double quick: very quickly
Dead March from Saul: a slow, elegiac march from the oratorio *Saul* by George Frederick Handel (1685–1759). It is customarily played at state military funerals
petty officers: a rank of soldier subordinate to the sergeant but superior to the private soldiers
surplice: a white linen vestment worn by a minister
this is no place for a man of your profession: a clergyman traditionally offers the comforts of religion to the condemned man. This clergyman, however, cannot offer Richard the proper comforts of *his* religion
will: life-force, spiritual energy and power
blasphemous nonsense: the Puritan quite correctly points out the discrepancy between theory and practice. Offering a man the comforts of a merciful God while murdering him is blasphemy
got up: put on, staged
Handel's music . . . piety: consistent with his objections to the meaningless forms of Mrs Dudgeon's religion, Dick clearly asserts that outward forms cannot be made to conceal inner realities
Man that is born of woman hath: words from the funeral service of the Church of England
'Thou shalt not kill': the fifth commandment. The Devil's Disciple quotes Scripture to silence the clergyman: beliefs must be stronger than the forms of words; if the clergyman believed the tenets of his own religion he could not participate in an execution
can no longer be inconvenienced by them: in other words, until after he is dead
to commit murder: Richard will not allow his executioners to cover their actions in false terminology but insists that murder is murder
what my commission cost me: officers had to buy their commissions into the army, the price varying from regiment to

regiment according to its status and reputation

in devilish bad part: with bad grace, with a lack of politeness

artful: clever

Fall back: retire from your position and go behind the lines (of soldiers)

pinions him: ties his arms together

chronometer: time-piece, watch

Amen! my life for the world's future: Richard's heroic last line was, in fact, changed from its original because the theatre manager considered 'Long live the devil and damn King George' was too offensive to an audience accustomed to patriotic melodrama

an American clock: Burgoyne urbanely implies that only clocks of British workmanship keep correct time

that American citizen: under his safe conduct pass Anderson is able to utter such a treasonable thought with impunity

the hour of trial: the time of great difficulty

his true profession: that which he really wishes to profess, to bear witness to

his destiny: the design of his life. Shaw believed that strong men, possessors of the life-force, were bound to pursue their destinies

Reverend Richard Dudgeon: for the sake of symmetry it is understandable why Shaw chose to include this unlikely reversal of roles. From the motivational point of view, however, there is little to indicate why this should happen. Richard has consistently used religion to point out the faults of his fellow men and in that sense he is a preacher. However, to imply that he could accept the orthodoxy of a Presbyterian ministry seems alien to what we know of the character

pow: head

saints as well as soldiers: Anderson is the soldier and Richard the saint, the person spurred on by a mission, a true Puritan

the British War Office: the British department of government which handled the affairs of war. In the case of the American revolution, orders from Britain took so long to arrive that they were often irrelevant by the time they did

quarters: barracks where the soldiers were housed

be d—: be damned

cock up your chins: put your chins in the air in a gesture of defiance

Slope arms!:   a military order to put guns at an angle on the shoulder

Fours!:   Form into lines of four

British Grenadiers: a famous British military march

Yankee Doodle: the rallying song of the American revolution and, consequently, highly offensive to British troops

Part 3

Commentary

The Devil's Disciple is a play of complex ideas and simple action; it is derived from many sources and yet is quintessentially Shavian. This commentary section deals with: (*a*) the secular and religious background to the play; (*b*) the particular theatrical ambience from which it emerged; (*c*) the philosophical and literary influences shown in the play; (*d*) the structure and language of the play itself.

Secular and religious background

The historical context

'Give me liberty, or give me death', the phrase used by the American revolutionist, Patrick Henry (1736–99), sums up the extreme longing for freedom which characterised the secession of the American colonies from the British Empire. America was, because of the nature of its foundation by those fleeing from religious intolerance, by adventurers and entrepreneurs, a land peopled by rugged individualists who grew increasingly disenchanted with rule from a parliament separated from it by culture as much as by distance. Increasingly, the vocabularies of the two countries drifted apart: 'power', 'authority', 'representation in government' meant different things to politicians on opposite sides of the Atlantic. As a consequence, colonial resentment at virtual non-representation in a body which legislated for, taxed and ruled America increased. The British government, motivated by crippling debts and a paternalistic desire to punish rebellious colonists, imposed stern measures: the Sugar Act (1764), the Currency Act (1764), the Stamp Act (1764), the Quartering Act (1765), the Tea Act (1773), the Coercive Acts (1774) were all designed to protect British interests at the expense of America. Their true effect, however, was to fuel the growing radical movement. Thomas Paine's *Common Sense*, published in 1776, articulated the need for secession, and the Declaration of Independence was made in the summer of the same year. The revolutionary war was not a major military contest since there were rarely more than 10,000 troops involved in one battle. However, the widely spread campaigns dragged on until 1781 when the disorganisation of British tactics together with the numerical superiority of the colonists eventually resulted in the

British surrender at Yorktown on 17 October, four years to the day after Burgoyne's defeat at Saratoga, the battle which he anticipates in *The Devil's Disciple*.

Shaw's theme of the conflict of a strongly individual man with secular and religious authority is one which achieves its ideal setting in the American War of Independence. The desire of the colonists was for self-government by a federation of individuals, a federation in which all beliefs were to be tolerated and all men were to have the right and the responsibility to pursue their individual courses for the common good. The desire of all Shaw's men of genius was similar: to find true liberty by assertion of individual will. In *The Eton Review* of March 1918, Shaw wrote words on the subject of individual liberty which illuminate the judgements of Anthony Anderson and Richard Dudgeon in *The Devil's Disciple*: 'Liberty is the right to think and choose for oneself. What liberty costs is the trouble of thinking and choosing for oneself. He who thinks liberty worth the trouble, and actually likes the trouble is the only really free . . . man.'

Puritanism

Puritanism was an extreme form of the Calvinist religion. It flourished in England during the sixteenth and seventeenth centuries and, following religious persecution there, became rooted in the New England settlements of America. From its origins as a pure form of worship which spurned excessive ornamentation of church buildings, of sacred music, of dress, which rejected mere emotionalism in worship, which advocated personal responsibility for salvation, it gradually altered to become a rigid orthodoxy covering social as well as religious behaviour. Puritanism held that man was essentially evil and that he could only be saved by the decision of a stern God who would, possibly, reward the good but who would, certainly, punish those who deviated from the narrow paths of righteousness. In other words, what began as an individual cry for personal freedom of worship and behaviour gradually became solidified into a repressive and negative social code. Both the individual cry and the repressive code are represented by the play's two Puritans: Richard Dudgeon and Mrs Dudgeon.

Mrs Dudgeon is a true representative of the outworn forms of a once-vital creed. In her, love is sacrificed to a duty which is cold and without charity. Repressive puritanical observance has so eliminated all feeling in her that when Anthony Anderson urges her to look into her heart to find grief she angrily rejects his advice: 'We are told that the heart of man is deceitful above all things, and desperately wicked . . . . Eli Hawkins . . . . warned me and strengthened me against my heart . . . . What else but that discipline has made me the woman I am?'

Such a discipline, of course stands condemned by the very character it has produced: Mrs Dudgeon. Nor did Shaw spare any effort to enable us to see Mrs Dudgeon and what she stands for as a negative force in the play. Consider the way she is described in stage directions: her face is '*grimly* trenched by the channels into which the *barren* forms and observances of a *dead* Puritanism can pen a *bitter temper* and a fierce pride'; she has a reputation for '*piety* and *respectability*' but it has gained her only '*dominion* and *detestation*' at home; she sits '*brooding* over her wrongs'; she speaks '*bitterly*' and '*sharply*' and calls in a '*hard, driving, wrathful* way,' and so on. She is, in fact, the play's central symbol of dead Puritanism so embalmed in outward forms that inner spiritual death goes unnoticed.

Richard Dudgeon, on the other hand, is a Puritan who is vitally alive. True to the original spirit of the religion, he is a man who longs for freedom of thought and of religious observation, who is intolerant of the imposition of negative and barren codes and one who belives in the rights of the individual and his ability to shape his own destiny. Richard's religion must come from a belief within himself; he will not accept beliefs which have been determined by others. Through the character of Richard, Shaw wishes to show how an individual of great spirit can reject the ghosts of the past; old beliefs cling like darkness, the new Puritan must let in the light. Mrs Alving in Ibsen's *Ghosts* captures Shaw's concept of the deadening effect of outworn ideas, concepts and creeds:

> Ghosts! . . . I almost believe we are all ghosts, Pastor Manders. It is not only what we have inherited from our fathers and mothers that walk on in us. It is every kind of dead idea, lifeless old beliefs and so on. They are not alive, but they cling to us for all that, and we can never rid ourselves of them. Whenever I read a newspaper I seem to see ghosts stealing between the lines. There must be ghosts the whole country over, as thick as the sands of the sea. And then we are all of us so wretchedly afraid of the light.

Shaw's true Puritans must let in the light and destroy the ghosts by a direct and clear-sighted pursuit of a 'master passion'.

In the character of Richard Dudgeon the 'master passion' is shown to be a desire for spiritual freedom sought in defiance of convention. Shaw explains Richard's Puritanism in his preface to the play: 'He is brought up in a household where the Puritan religion has died, and become, in its corruption, an excuse for his mother's master passion of hatred in all its phases of cruelty and envy . . . . In such a home the young Puritan finds himself starved of religion, which is the most clamorous need of his nature. With all his mother's indomitable self-fulness, but with Pity instead of Hatred as his master passion, he pities the devil; takes his side; and champions him, like a true Covenanter, against the world. He thus becomes, like all genuinely religious men, a reprobate and an outcast.' Richard Dudgeon, then, is the central symbol of vital Puritanism. Contrasting sharply with his mother, with the ironically named Christy, and with his vapid relatives, Richard may be seen as a force of positive energy, a character in whom will freely determines belief and action.

Theatrical background

Tradition and experimentation

When Shaw began to write for the London theatre, fashionable taste favoured either melodrama, at its best perhaps in the plays of Dion Boucicault (1822–90), or romantic social comedy which reached its highest point in the plays of Oscar Wilde (1854–1900). Elsewhere, however, drama had begun to move in new and challenging directions. Designed to educate rather than to entertain, to provoke rather than to please, the new dramatic style had many enemies both among the public and the critics. Works by August Strindberg (1849–1912), Anton Chekov (1860–1904) and Ibsen were either dismissed as sordid or refused permission for public performance on the grounds that they corrupted the morals of those who witnessed them. Ibsen's *Ghosts*, for example, which was performed in London in 1891, was seen as 'an open drain; a loathsome sore unbandaged; a dirty act done publicly'.

The drama of Henrik Ibsen, the target of such abuse, was one of the most potent influences on the writings of Shaw and, indeed, on much of twentieth-century drama. Ibsen moved dramatic writing away from stock situations, cardboard characters and complicated plots and placed new emphasis on the subtle psychological drama of characters placed in difficult but recognisable situations. False religions, false relationships based on social convention rather than individual conviction, freedom of women, freedom of youth from the restricting bonds of outworn ideas, all provided the thematic material for Ibsen's plays while the sufferings of those trapped by society provided material for character depth and psychological realism. Ibsen's drama was not bounded by realism; his works often fit with difficulty into the conventional dramatic form and become more like music. But it was Ibsen's realistic plays which most influenced Shaw, and his essay *The Quintessence of Ibsenism* (1890) underlies his indebtedness to them. Ibsen emphasised the subject rather than mode, and this was in accordance with Shaw's own developing ideas about the nature and purpose of dramatic art.

In *The Devil's Disciple* Shaw exploits both the popular and the experimental fashions of his time, merging Ibsen's theme of the dilemma of moral choice with the plot of a conventional melodrama.

Melodrama

Melodrama was the most popular dramatic form in the nineteenth century. It was largely a drama of situation in which a fast moving plot was acted out by predictable stock characters in stock situations. Spectacle, too, was a necessary part of this genre and many melodramas contained such elaborate tricks of staging as shipwrecks, earthquakes and horse-racing. The dramatic emphasis was on the arousal of emotions in the audience, and whether the emotion was pity, terror, admiration or patriotism it had to satisfy the moral requirements of the audience: virtue always had to triumph over evil.

The Adelphi Theatre in London's Strand was the most famous of the theatres specialising in melodrama, and Shaw paid his first visit to the Adelphi shortly after he became drama reviewer for *The Saturday Review* in 1895. In his review, he commented: 'As a superior person . . . I hold the Adelphi melodrama in high consideration. A really good Adelphi melodrama is of first-rate literary importance, because it only needs elaboration to become a masterpiece'. In the same review he went on to define the characteristics of a good melodrama, characteristics which he, as 'a superior person', would use to turn this form into a masterpiece:

> It should be a simple and sincere drama of action and feeling, kept well within that vast tract of passion and motive which is common to the philosopher and the labourer, relieved by plenty of fun, and depending for variety of human character, not on the high comedy idiosyncrasies which individualise people in spite of the closest similarity of age, sex and circumstance, but on broad contrasts between types of youth and age, sympathy and selfishness, the masculine and the feminine, the sublime and the ridiculous, and so on. The whole character of the piece must be allegorical, idealistic, full of generalisations and moral lessons; and it must represent conduct as producing swiftly and certainly on the individual the results which in actual life it only produces on the race in the course of many centuries.

Shaw's requirements of the melodramatic form were, then, as follows: (*a*) a simplicity of action, plot and characterisation; (*b*) a delineation of characters based on broad contrasts of attitude rather than subtleties of motivation; (*c*) a didactic content in which retribution or reward is seen to be immediate and just.

And how far does *The Devil's Disciple* fulfil the requirements of melodrama? The plot is simple: mistaken identity and heroic sacrifice constituted a familiar pattern, its most famous use being in Dickens's *A Tale of Two Cities* (1859) which was dramatised by Tom Taylor in 1860. The set-piece scenes of melodrama are all present: the prodigal's return, the trial, the execution, the timely rescue. The characterisation is broad and such subtleties of motivation as do appear are unsatisfactory: Dick's reason for his sacrifice and his silence, his suggested change to a parson at the end, lack any depth of textual motivation. The didactic message—man must be free to follow his own destiny—is heavily underscored, and retribution and reward are meted out in a totally traditional fashion. In short, were it not for the sharpness of the dialogue and the irony of the dramatist's vision *The Devil's Disciple* might be, in Shaw's own words, 'exposed as the threadbare popular melodrama it technically is'.

Boucicault's *Arrah-Na-Pogue*

The plot of *The Devil's Disciple* leans heavily on one of the most popular melodramas of the Victorian Age: Boucicault's *Arrah-Na-Pogue* (1864). There are many similarities between the two plays: each is set against the background of a struggle for political freedom—in Boucicault's case this is the Irish fight for independence from Britain in 1798; because of a mistaken identity the wrong man is condemned to be executed; the pretty heroine loses faith in her lover because she thinks, incorrectly, that he has acted in a cowardly way; there is a trial during which the accused man jokes lightheartedly with his captors; the heroine faints when her lover is arrested; a kindly sergeant is sympathetic to the lovers but feels he has to do his duty; there is a stereotype military man who believes in the rule of military discipline over mere human feelings.

Thematically, too, there is a relationship between the two plays: conviction, they would seem to argue, is not the same as passion. Those who emerge as heroes are those guided by passion, the rest are imaginatively restricted by their convictions of rectitude and duty. Shaw's attitude towards the stultifying effect of religion or political conviction is very close to that expressed in the words of Boucicault's Colonel O'Grady on the military stereotype, Major Coffin:

> There goes a kind-hearted gentleman, who would cut more throats on principle and firm conviction than another blackguard would sacrifice to the worst passions of his nature. If there is one thing that misleads a man more than another thing it is having a firm conviction about anything.

Both plays deal with decisions made against a threatening background of an alien military presence. In such a tense atmosphere as that generated by the American or the Irish Rebellion a simple action or decision can have disproportionate consequences. However, although Shaw draws heavily on the mechanics of Boucicault's play, he moves from a conventional melodramatic stance in his handling of the theme, making educational, political and social comment through the delineation of his characters and by what they say and do.

Philosophical and literary influences

The Marriage of Heaven and Hell

The poet William Blake (1757–1827) was a mystic who created his own mode of looking at man's spiritual existence. Orthodox Christianity Blake found to be inadequate since, as he saw it, it had become perverted through the activities of its institutions, the churches. As one of the earliest exponents of Romanticism in English poetry, Blake sought to express the power, majesty and magnitude of the spirit of each individual man: wide-ranging spiritual freedom was a necessity for the growth of each soul; the churches sought to curtail that freedom and stunt the growth of the soul.

In his strange poem *The Marriage of Heaven and Hell* Blake argues that the opposition between Heaven and Hell, good and evil, is merely a distortion of the truth which is that both are necessary to the spiritual well-being of man. They are vital contraries not opposites: 'Without Contraries', wrote Blake, 'is no progression. Attraction and Repulsion, Reason and Energy, Love and Hate, are necessary to Human existence.' Energy is the true dominating force in man and man must follow his desires or lose himself. The poem inverts our normal expectations that heaven and God are good, and hell and Satan are bad. In it heaven is seen as the seat of Reason and restraint, a stultifying and oppressive force, whereas hell is a place of energy and desire, a creative and positive force. Hell, the abode of Satan the devil, is the home of necessary revolution, a truly spiritual place where the conventions of an oppressive God have to be overthrown. Shaw's Richard Dudgeon is certainly a disciple of this devil as is his *alter ego*, Anthony Anderson. Consider the following selection of Blake's Proverbs of Hell (in *The Marriage of Heaven and Hell*) in the light of Shaw's play:

> Drive your cart and your plow over the bones of the dead.
> The road of excess leads to the palace of wisdom.
> He who desires but acts not breeds pestilence.
> The most sublime act is to set another before you.

Prisons are built with the stones of Law, Brothels with
   bricks of Religion.
The bird a nest, the spider a web, man friendship.
The tygers of wrath are wiser than the horses of instruction.

In his preface to *Three Plays for Puritans* (1901) Shaw acknowledges
his debt to Blake's ideas: 'Let those who have praised my originality in
conceiving Dick Dudgeon's strange religion read Blake's *Marriage of
Heaven and Hell* and I shall be fortunate if they do not rail at me for a
plagiarist.'

The 'life-force' and the Superman

Many of Shaw's later heroes are supermen, men so driven by the 'life-
force' within them that they place themselves outside the normal moral
judgements of good and evil. The 'life-force' which was to become a
most important term in Shaw's philosophy was derived from the idea
of 'Will' in the philosophy of Artur Schopenhauer (1788–1860) and
the *élan vital* of Henri Bergson (1859–1941). Don Juan in Shaw's *Man
and Superman* (1901–3) explains the workings of the life-force within
him:

   I can tell you as long as I can conceive something better than myself I
   cannot be easy unless I am striving to bring it into existence or
   clearing the way for it. That is the law of my life. That is the working
   within me of Life's incessant aspiration to higher organisation,
   wider, deeper, intenser self-consciousness, and clearer self-under-
   standing.

The philosophy which suggests that there is such a person as a superman is derived from the works of Friedrich Nietzsche (1844–1900). In
Thus Spoke Zarathustra (1883), Nietzsche prophesied the coming of a
superman, the *Herrenmensch*, who was a law unto himself, and put
forward the theory that the meaning of history is in the rare but bril-
liant appearances of exceptional individuals. While the philosophy of a
superman and the demands of his life-force as they appear in *The
Devil's Disciple* have not the intellectual clarity they later achieved in
Shaw's work, they are inherent in the characters of Anderson and
Richard Dudgeon. Both, in striving to bring something more
important than themselves into existence, declare they have performed
these actions according to the law of their natures. The urge to follow a
specific destiny spurred on by the urgings of a natural instinct and a
fierce will is the primary motivating force of their actions. Each is in
fact, an embryonic superman, 'being used for a purpose recognised by
yourself as a mighty one' (Preface to *Man and Superman*).

The structure and language of the play

Character grouping

Each major theme in the play is encapsulated in a struggle between carefully balanced characters.

(*a*) Prayer *vs.* Action. At first this struggle seems a straightforward conflict between the satanic man of action, Richard Dudgeon, and the man of God, Anthony Anderson, and their reversal of roles at the end simply an illustration of the theory that any emotion strongly felt can quickly become its opposite. By allowing us to hear Richard's reasoning, however, and by the introduction of the character of Burgoyne, the rational man of thought, Shaw suggests that it is neither good nor evil which is the ultimate goal but intellect, the power to reason and to make an informed choice. The attitude of Burgoyne—and Shaw—is best expressed in William Blake's *Jerusalam*:

> I care not whether a Man is Good or Evil; all that I care
> Is whether he is a Wise Man or a Fool. Go! put off Holiness,
> And put on Intellect.

(*b*) Emotion *vs.* Desire. Judith Anderson is at the centre of this conflict. Intellectually committed to a man of prayer she is more deeply attracted to a man of action. The triangle which develops is similar to to that in Shaw's *Candida*, where the heroine is trapped between a dreamer and a determined man. Judith does not seem to matter very much to either man and her weakly emotional fickleness is disposed of quite casually in the end. The two men recognise the common strength of their vocations, their desires and destinies; emotionalism is irrelevant to their strength of purpose.

(*c*) Invididual *vs.* Society. The demands of society are presented in the characters of Mrs Dudgeon and General Burgoyne, representing religious and political duty respectively. Each voices the demands of the *status quo*: religious observation is good, satanism is bad; colonial government is necessary, revolution means treachery. Richard Dudgeon is the individual driven by the law of his own nature who is pitted against these forces. The individual exposes the flaws in outworn ideas and lays bare the fundamental injustice of imposed societal norms.

(*d*) Natural *vs.* Unnatural. The natural world is presented in the character of Essie, the unnatural in that of Mrs Dudgeon. All Essie's actions and responses show a natural humanity and mobility of spirit against which the actions of Mrs Dudgeon appear as warped and distorted Christianity. Richard is the champion of the natural forces as is seen by his action at the end of Act I. This conflict does not disappear, however, with the absence of Mrs Dudgeon in subsequent acts; her place is taken by Judith Anderson, and Essie remains, with her simple loyalties truly observed, as a commentary on and a challenge to the 'unnatural' egotism of Judith.

(e) The clash of duties. You will have noticed how many times the characters in this play use the term 'duty'. The conflict arises because these duties are mutually exclusive. Mrs Dudgeon has a duty to conform to her religion; Judith is duty-bound to observe her promises to Anderson and to Richard; Anderson has a duty to his parishioners which conflicts with his duty to his country, and so on. It is Burgoyne who exposes the folly of mindless adherence to duty in his sarcastic undermining of Major Swindon's reliance on the formula that every man will do his duty. Doing his duty does not 'throw a flood of light on the situation', only honest intellectual appraisal will do that.

Language

The language of the play may be seen to express a conflict between religious and military vocabulary. 'Sin' and 'shame' are established at the outset as part of Mrs Dudgeon's religion and her discussion on grief with Anderson uses scriptural quotation in such close proximity with words of hate and anger that the audience is quickly able to gauge the quality of her religious fervour. Richard Dudgeon also uses much scriptural quotation, sarcastically at times, but also particularly in pointing out the inadequacies of orthodox Christian teaching; for example, his direct challenge, 'Thou shalt not kill', to the military chaplain effectively silences this clergyman, a man of God who is party to a killing. The military vocabulary in the play is not used simply by the soldiers, although it incidentally has the effect of keeping their presence in our minds. It is also used by and about Anderson, thus implanting the suggestion that he is something of a military figure despite appearances to the contrary.

The single strongly individual voice among the characters is that of Burgoyne. Presented as a man of style and wit Burgoyne is given Shaw's choicest epigrams: 'Martydom, sir, is what these people like: it is the only way a man can become famous without ability', or 'I do not express my opinion. I never stoop to that habit of profane language which unfortunately coarsens our profession'. His presence on stage also seems to bring out the acerbic wit in the language of Richard Dudgeon, although his is not a cultivated or refined wit but one born of a sharp decisiveness. The sophisticated style of Burgoyne serves to highlight the puritanical sparseness of much of the rest of the language. Perhaps Shaw attempted to invert Wilde's epigram: 'In matters of grave importance, style, not sincerity, is the vital thing.' In a play for Puritans, sincerity had to be 'the vital thing'.

Part 4

Hints for study

Approaching a dramatic text

When you read the text of a play you see only part of its art at work. A truly dramatic work only achieves life when the words are spoken by living people, when the clash of temperaments and ideas appears before us in flesh and blood, when set and lights create a scene before our eyes, and the whole magic of theatre breathes life into the play. A play text is like a painter's cartoon, an indication of the potential work but not the work itself. Accordingly, you should read a dramatic text using your imagination to the full, creating the characters, the setting, the sound and the movements in the theatre of your mind. This is not always easy and Shaw, in particular, was conscious of the missing links, supplied on stage by the imagination of actors and directors, with which the reader would find difficulty. He, therefore, approached the publication of a play-text almost as another author would approach his novel, providing character notes and elaborate descriptions of settings so that the reader could re-create more easily the atmosphere of Shaw's ideal performance.

A sound familiarity with the dramatic text is a first requirement when studying a play such as *The Devil's Disciple*, and the dramatic text in this case includes the character notes and the stage directions. From this familiarity you will gain a clear knowledge of the characters, their interactions and the tensions between them. A sense of the characters developing through the action of the plot leads inevitably to a consideration of the themes they embody in their speech and actions. If you follow this approach you should be able to tackle any question on the text with confidence, knowing your own familiarity with the dramatic trinity: character, action, speech.

Answering questions on *The Devil's Disciple*

In answering any literary question you must be aware that the examiner is looking for a shaped response with a beginning, middle and end. He is interested not merely in how well you know the text but also in how you can formulate a coherent response to his question. You should, accordingly, select and emphasise. Select the examples and ideas most relevant to the answer; emphasise whatever approach or answer to the question you find most stimulating. This will lead to a structured response with a focus which gives it interest and direction. Introduce, develop and conclude. The introduction should answer the question and indicate the direction of the argument, the middle paragraphs develop the important strands of the argument, while the final paragraph should conclude the argument by restating the answer, an answer now proved to be valid. By following this basic structure you should be able to interest the examiner in your approach and show both familiarity with the text and ability to shape ideas.

Questions on drama generally fall into four categories. In the first there are questions relating to the historical or genre background to the play, how a writer did or did not use the fashionable methods of his day. Into the second come questions on characterisation. In the third questions may be asked on the thematic content of the work including its relation to the author's philosophy. The fourth category may pose questions on the language of the play, the writer's individual style and techniques. Sometimes a question may combine two or more of these categories and your response must be adjusted accordingly. However, a consideration of these four categories should help you to formulate general guidelines for your response which can then be modified to suit particular questions.

Questions about historical or genre background

'*The Devil's Disciple* blends the ideas of Ibsen with the most successful theatrical formula of the nineteenth century: the melodrama.' Comment on this evaluation of the play.

When approaching questions such as this you should consider both the play and the background or stylistic tradition from which it emerged. Therefore, you should: (*a*) know something of the theatrical context of the play, the styles and conventions of theatre which were popular at the time of writing; (*b*) find out what was the author's attitude towards these conventions and whether or not he was an experimental writer; (*c*) consider how the author used the conventions of his day, whether he used them to satirise or to be serious; (*d*) illustrate how the particular play uses the styles and conventions you have discovered. For example, the question above assumes that you have learnt something about the conventions of melodrama, have investigated the emerging influence of Ibsen on dramatists concerned with social and political issues, and that you can see how the older convention of melodrama is modified by inclusion of some of the themes or techniques encouraged by the new writers.

Sample question and answer: Shaw referred to *The Devil's Disciple* as 'a threadbare popular melodrama'. How far may the play be considered a conventional melodrama?

Melodrama, the most popular form of drama in the nineteenth century, was distinguished by a broad and formulaic handling of character and action; its characters were stock characters and its situations stock situations. It thrived on sensational happenings and on the arousal of the audience's emotions of hate, pity or admiration. While melodrama was, at its best, exciting theatre, it was not a subtle form. George Bernard Shaw, on the other hand, was a subtle dramatist who wished to educate and reform his audiences by encouraging their rational rather than their emotional responses. In writing *The Devil's Disciple* he wished to challenge his audience's expectations, to arouse their rational responses to religious and social issues. However, he wanted to achieve this in its most palatable form and to that end he used the external conventions of melodramatic characters and situations imposed on a thematic framework of religious, political and social seriousness.

The characters step straight out of conventional melodrama. There is a hero seemingly given to evil but concealing within his black heart a core of purest gold. There is a fainting heroine who discovers she is swayed by passion she cannot control, an upright man who is a true patriot, a nasty old person who resents the behaviour of the young. As in melodrama, the characters are rewarded or punished according to their just deserts: Mrs Dudgeon dies, Richard is vindicated, Anderson finds his true vocation and Judith is shown to be a pretty fool. However, the characters and their activities are not as straightforward as the above implies. Both Richard Dudgeon and Anthony Anderson are early attempts by Shaw to dramatise the life-force which he felt to be present in every man of genius. Richard Dudgeon through his diabolism inverts the audience's expectations of good and evil: we recognise that the Devil's Disciple is good and that conventional good is mere restriction and loss of positive energies. All the main characters are faced not with melodramatic obstacles but with deeply moral dilemmas which they must resolve within themselves. In short, the characterisation is a complex mixture of melodramatic and Ibsenite styles, an unusual if not a unique combination.

The plot, too, seems to follow a conventional melodramatic pattern: the mistaken identity, the lovers' meeting before the trial, the trial scene itself, the spectacular execution. Shaw has, however, so constructed and set the plot that the moral difficulties and problems of the central characters are thrown into sharp relief by the situations and settings in which they find themselves. Thus, the mistaken arrest of Richard Dudgeon poses for the audience not the simple melodramatic problem of how the wrong man could be arrested but the moral problem of how far a man may take a decision of his own will; the change of Parson Anderson into Captain Anderson serves not only as a neat plot reversal but as a question to the audience on the relative value of prayer and action. In other words, while using a conventional structure Shaw highlights the points of moral dilemma of his characters and forces the audience to make a rational assessment of the characters' responses to those dilemmas.

Religious, social and political issues form the thematic net of the play. The conflict between the new and the old Puritanism is presented so that we are made aware of the value of individual spirituality. The presentation of patriotism under both its idealistic and realistic guises asks us to question how far a man should take duty to his country as duty to his fellow men. We see that the demands of society, seen in the imposition of the religious and political *status quo*, are false and inadequate. Therefore, we may conclude that the thematic considerations of the play are far more complex and difficult than those of a conventional melodrama.

The Devil's Disciple is a melodrama, but it is the melodrama of a subtle man.

Questions on characterisation

(i) Consider the characterisation of Anthony Anderson as a man of prayer and a man of action.

(ii) Judith Anderson is a pawn in the serious game between Richard Dudgeon and Anthony Anderson. Discuss.

This type of question is deceptively simple. It does *not* ask you to give a description of a character as if he or she was a real person. Rather it asks that you appreciate how the author has manipulated words, actions and patterns of behaviour into a dramatic unit which is credible; for example, there is no such person as Richard Dudgeon, the character is a dramatic illusion created by Shaw. Without labouring the point, it is essential when answering a question on character that you remain aware of character as one of the elements of artistic creation. So, approach a question on characterisation with great care and formulate your preliminary work from three standpoints: (*a*) consider how each of the central characters is presented in terms of what he does, what he says, how he reacts to others, what he says about himself, what others say about him, and, with Shaw's works, how he is described by the author; (*b*) familiarise yourself with character groupings within the play, noting whether a character is balanced by another or stands out as unique; (c) consider whether or not a character is in some sense symbolic, that is, whether or not he has a meaning ancillary to the apparent surface one. From a judicious selection of material so discovered you should be able to approach a question of this type with confidence. Above all, however, stay objective: liking or disliking a character is a subjective emotional response which, while it might be valid for viewing the play in the theatre, is of little use in formulating a critical response.

Sample question and answer: Consider the character of Richard Dudgeon as the 'Puritan of Puritans'.

While at first glance it may seem strange for the author of *The Devil's Disciple* to describe his satanic hero as 'the Puritan of Puritans', on further consideration one is forced to admit that Richard Dudgeon is, in fact, more of a Puritan than those who claim to belong to that religious sect. And what exactly is a Puritan? A Puritan is one who holds to the purity of his religion. He rejects false images, despises excess of ornamentation and emotion, and so believes in the validity of his own faith that he is willing to suffer exile or even death in order to preserve it. The false Puritans of the play maintain the external forms of a once vital religion but spiritually they are desiccated and mistrustful of the life force of others. Richard Dudgeon, on the other hand, is true to the pure moral law of his own nature and suffers in defence of his religion.

Through his use of the character of Richard Dudgeon, Shaw shows the effects of placing an anarchist in a settled and complacent society: he challenges its assumptions and destabilises it. Although it would have been historically inaccurate to place the popular anarchic doctrines of Mikhail Bakunin (1814–76) and Peter Kropotkin (1842–1921) in the mouth of a character 'living' in 1777, Shaw uses a form of the anarchists' doctrines to voice his own challenge to society. Anarchists believed that all men, though essentially good, were perverted by the social institutions they themselves initiated. They further held that it was only by constant challenging of the social system that true freedom of the individual could be achieved. That such a doctrine could be associated with the American Revolution is quite credible, since the aim of the colonists was to achieve a confederation of self-determining individuals motivated by ideals of communal responsibility. That such a doctrine could be associated with Puritanism is also quite credible, since the original aim of the Puritans was to cleanse society of its impurities and challenge its religious complacency. So, how is Richard Dudgeon shown as an anarchic Puritan? He challenges the efficacy of his family's religion, he causes Anderson to reassess the value of his ministry and Judith to reassess the value of her marriage. He questions the validity of Burgoyne's presence in his country and the empty ritualising of murder. By doing this he questions the fundamental structures of society: religion, politics and marriage. Shaw uses the character, therefore, as a catalyst to begin the questioning of the false images, false ideals which beset society.

Like a true Puritan, too, Richard Dudgeon despises excess, particularly excess of emotion. He is rational in his actions and judgements, making decisions based on reasoning rather than emotion. Thus he is shown strongly repudiating Judith's notion that he acted out of love of her: 'What I did last night, I did in cold blood.' Any judgement made under the stress of emotion is automatically suspect: Richard Dudgeon sets 'very little store by the goodness that only comes out red hot'. In his mistrust of emotion, he shows his parentage: his mother, too, despised action dictated by the heart rather than the mind. His rational Puritanical decisions, however, are made by positive rather than negative responses to his fellow men. Richard Dudgeon acts according to his belief in his own nature and his responsibility towards others. He demonstrates, in short, the necessity for the informed individual conscience which was the basis of Puritanism.

Finally, the determined will to express his religion which characterises all true Puritans is also a characteristic of Richard Dudgeon. The character is, in fact, one of Shaw's early studies of individuals motivated by what he termed a 'life-force', a single burning energy which turns such men into men of genius above and beyond the normal moral and social codes. Richard Dudgeon is motivated by a burning zeal to reform, and Shaw carefully places suggestions of the religious zeal with which he follows his vocation: 'I do not interfere with your sermons: do not you interrupt mine', he orders Anderson; he is shown ruthlessly exposing the unchristian nature of the treatment of Essie, the hypocrisy of a rigged trial, the blasphemy of offering a condemned man the 'comforts' of religion. Furthermore, Shaw gives Richard Dudgeon many biblical and scriptural quotations which, used by the character in an ironic context, show up the fundamental flaws in the false religion of the others.

The final change which Shaw proposed—the reversal of the roles of Parson and Devil's Disciple—is, therefore, a simple dramatic device to underline what has been made clear right through the play: that the Devil's Disciple is 'the Puritan of Puritans'.

Questions on language and style

To answer questions in this category you must know the text of the play very well indeed because you must use precise and aptly chosen quotations to substantiate your answers. Having familiarised yourself with the text in general you should then pick out (*a*) images or uses of language which are most characteristic of the play and (*b*) stylistic devices which are peculiar to the author. In this play, for example, there is a very clear usage of both military and religious language, while the characteristic epigrams and balanced sentences of Shaw are to be found particularly in the language of Burgoyne and Richard Dudgeon. However, when you have traced the patterns of the language and chosen your examples, you must avoid the temptation of simply displaying your knowledge to the examiner. Use your information to make a clearly constructed response to the question: illustration only illustrates when it is throwing light on some carefully considered point.

Sample question and answer: '*The Devil's Disciple* relies heavily on the language of the Bible'. Consider the implications of Shaw's reliance on this source.

The Devil's Disciple is quite clearly a play about Puritanism and as such it is appropriate that it should use the language of the religion in question. The way in which Shaw uses this language, however, is not straightforward. In fact, Shaw through his use of biblical and scriptural language calls into question the validity of that religion. With the exception of Burgoyne, all the main characters use religious language but they condemn religion either, as in Richard Dudgeon's case, by ironic use of phrases revered by others, or, as in Mrs Dudgeon's case, through what they reveal about their own religious responses.

Shaw makes Mrs Dudgeon reveal the fundamental emptiness of her convictions by the close juxtaposition of religious quotation and secular hatred. Consider the following examples:

ANDERSON Sister, the Lord has laid his hand very heavily on you.
MRS DUDGEON... It's His will, I suppose; and I must bow to it. But I do think it hard. What call had Timothy to go to Springtown, and remind everybody that he belonged to a man that was being hanged?—and (*spitefully*) that deserved it, if ever a man did.

or

ANDERSON Well, Richard's earthly father has been merciful to him; and his heavenly judge is the father of us all.
MRS DUDGEON... Richard's earthly father was a softheaded—

In the first example the pious, if clichéd, comfort offered by Anderson is met at first with a similarly pious, if clichéd response: 'It's His will'. However, the piety is immediately undermined by the tentative 'I suppose', and while it returns for an instant in 'I must bow to it', any doubts as to Mrs Dudgeon's 'Christian' feelings are dispelled by her personal horror that she has been socially compromised, and her outrageous sense of religious superiority is shown in her judgement of her brother-in-law's deserts. By this juxtaposition of piety and hate, Shaw has cleverly allowed Mrs Dudgeon to be condemned out of her own mouth, displaying her greater concern for her own social and religious superiority than for any compassion or pious acceptance. The second example shows a similar pattern. Once again Anderson offers the conventional vocabulary and response to Mrs Dudgeon's desire for the punishment of Richard's 'wickedness'. This time, however, Mrs Dudgeon does not waste time replying in Anderson's vocabulary but, according to the stage direction, *forgetting herself*, she indulges in a colloquial spurt of hatred. By such means Shaw allows the audience to judge Mrs Dudgeon as an exponent of a religion motivated by hate and duty rather than love, an empty religion which acts only as a negative force, restricting and confining, never growing.

Opposed to this empty religion Shaw has placed the character of Richard Dudgeon, who, by using a similar vocabulary and phrasing in an ironic context forces the other characters—and the audience—to appreciate the hollowness of a religion followed through duty rather than desire. 'My father died without the consolations of the law', he tells Hawkins, implying through the perversion of the usual phrase, 'the consolations of religion', that law and religion are on a par, both capable of corruption by an impure society. 'For what we are about to receive, may the Lord make us truly thankful', he quips before Hawkins reads the will, suggesting that the distribution of property to the gathered relatives is somewhat akin to the eating of a meal, both being equally blessed by a religion which confuses social and spiritual issues. 'Thou shalt not kill', he retorts to the Chaplain's hurried start to the funeral service, sharply pointing to the irony of using words of spiritual peace in the course of legalised murder. Richard Dudgeon's use of religious language acts as the conscience of the play, highlighting his moral actions outside the convention moral code by drawing attention to the hollow quality of the religious verbiage used by others.

And what of the language of that religious man, Anthony Anderson? Anderson's language exhibits the same tension as is evidenced in his character, the tension between his military and his religious vocations. Anderson's first words of religious comfort are somewhat clichéd; unlike any true minister, he does not attempt to speak to Mrs Dudgeon in terms she understands but rather imposes his vocabulary and judgement, the judgement of a man who followed his heart in his marriage. From the beginning of Act II Shaw begins to eliminate Anderson's religious phraseology in favour of a more direct type of speech, occasionally spiced by a military vocabulary: 'Do you think,' he asks, using a soldier's image, 'it would be better to know that I have run away from my post at the first sign of danger?' In this way, the language prepares us for the transition of Anderson from parson into 'a choleric and formidable man of war'. He rejects his former vocation: 'Pray! Can we pray Swindon's rope off Richard's neck?' Refuge in prayer is only a self-deception practised by those unwilling to act. 'God may soften Major Swindon's heart', suggests Judith, but Anderson's retort lays bare the inadequacy of reliance on heavenly intervention: 'I am not God; and I must go to work another way'. By changing Anderson's vocabulary during the play Shaw underscores the necessary elimination of religion from any plan of action. Through the character of Anderson Shaw suggests that conventional religion is a curtain behind which a man can hide only until he has found the spiritual force which makes him unique.

The use of so much religious language in *The Devil's Disciple* is one of Shaw's techniques for drawing attention to the religious questioning he proposes. Conventional religious observance like conventional religious phraseology is empty and meaningless. Only an individual mind, reasoning clearly and convinced of its own spiritual worth, can articulate a religious language with conviction and true worth.

Questions on thematic content

Questions of a thematic nature presuppose (*a*) that you know the text, (*b*) that you have decided for yourself what the play is about, (*c*) that you have considered the opinions of others as to the meaning of the play, (*d*) that you can separate the different thematic strands of the play and (*e*) that you can formulate a coherent response to the question. In general, this type of question requires you to take a stance on the subject: mere information will not suffice, you must also demonstrate your ability to argue a case. Therefore, once you have decided what information and illustration are relevant to the question you should try to structure your answer in the form of an argument. To do this you must first decide on the thesis of your argument; that is, on a concise statement of your basic answer. A statement of this thesis and an indication of what direction the argument intends to take should form the basis of your first paragraph. Three to four middle paragraphs, each taking a single point which is evidence for your thesis, will establish the validity of your argument. At this point it may be necessary to introduce whatever reservations or objections might be proposed to your thesis. Handle these carefully and do not allow them to outweigh your own points. Finally, your last paragraph should conclude by restating your thesis in the light of all the evidence you have adduced in its support. By following such a pattern as this you will construct a sharply observed, concise answer and will avoid the main pitfall of the thematic answer: vague rambling discourse about the plot. Selected evidence, pointed illustration and sound argument are your vital tools in answering the thematic question.

Sample question and answer: 'To be moral each individual must first be free.' Examine the treatment of this theme in *The Devil's Disciple*.

The Devil's Disciple is essentially a study of the necessity for and the responsibility of personal freedom. Freedom in the play is threatened from three sides: by state, religion and by dependence on others. Shaw attempts to show that in order to make a fully informed decision about his own destiny a man must first liberate himself from the ties of King, of God and of Kin.

By choosing as his setting the American War of Independence Shaw acted on his audience's awareness of the call for liberty and statehood, the primary objectives of the colonists, and thereby underlined the search for individual liberty which is at the core of the characters of Richard Dudgeon and Anthony Anderson. Society, Shaw believed, should be based on a federation of strong individuals all of whom knew that freedom meant more than simply shaking off the yoke of colonial oppression: freedom also entailed a responsibility to act for the common good. The American colonists had views similar to Shaw's: a strong desire to control their own destiny and a fundamental distaste for oppressive rule. The setting of the play, therefore—the struggle for independence of one state from another—acts as a huge mirror, magnifying the individual struggles of the central characters for personal liberty into an epic fight for national liberty. Anderson and Dudgeon both choose to reject the oppression of the British Crown, proudly proclaiming American citizenship even at the risk of their lives.

Choosing to die offers a man freedom from the tyranny of the fear of death; choosing to risk his soul frees him from the tyranny of religion. Religion of the orthodox kind is seen as a negative force in the play. Like unlawful government, it oppresses and stultifies a man's ability to judge and to act. In short, if a man adheres to the dictates of one religion to the exclusion of personal judgement he is not acting in a moral way. To highlight the tyrannous power of religion Shaw chose to make his hero an energetic satanist who espoused the freedom of Satan who declared to God: 'I will not serve'. Dick Dudgeon, having rejected the religion which made his mother and family what they are, is a truly moral man who can make his own decisions on how he should act. In doing this he is acting according to 'the law of his own nature', the starting point for the moral decisions of any free man. Anderson too must sell 'his family bible for a brace of pistols' in order to discover the true law of his nature.

If he throws off the shackles of oppressive government and religion is a man then completely free? Shaw would answer no. A man is still tied by those who, lacking his ability to choose and his will to decide, cling to his strength. To illustrate this final tie, Shaw created the character of Judith Anderson. Strength attracts Judith: like a pin to a magnet she is drawn first to one man and then to another as their strengths become apparent to her. She sees herself as a crucial element in their decisions but is fundamentally irrelevant to them: Richard is 'revolted' by her assumption that he acted out of love for her; Anderson tells her that she is 'a fool' not to know the man to whom she is married. Shaw demonstrates that mere sentimentality and emotionalism cloud moral issues and that decisions of fundamental importance must be reached by a rational mind unhampered by ties of love or emotion.

Through the characters of Richard Dudgeon and Anthony Anderson, through its setting during the American War of Independence, through its atmosphere of oppressive Puritanism, *The Devil's Disciple* creates an ambience in which Shaw can examine the theme of the moral nature of personal liberty, its necessity and its responsibilities.

Part 5

Suggestions for further reading

The text

There are many fine editions of Shaw's plays including the early ones which were approved by the author himself (see p.13). A useful paperback edition is published by Longman, with an introduction and notes by A.C. Ward, London, 1964.

Background reading

BLAKE, WILLIAM: *The Marriage of Heaven and Hell*, which can be found in any collection of Blake's work, is a valuable aid in appreciating Richard Dudgeon's satanism.
BOUCICAULT, DION: *Arrah-Na-Pogue*. This play provided Shaw with several of the plot details for his own work. It is also an example of typical melodramatic style. Available in an edition published by The Dolmen Press, Dublin, edited by David Krause.

Life of Shaw

There is no definitive life of Shaw available at present and early attempts have been outdated. *Bernard Shaw: A Chronicle* by R.F. Rattray, Haskell House, New York, 1982, is useful in establishing what Shaw did when, though its format is not that of a biography. Shaw on Shaw is most illuminating: try *Sixteen Self-Sketches*, Constable, London, 1949.

General studies with commentaries on *The Devil's Disciple*

COMPTON, LOUIS: *Shaw the Dramatist*, Allen and Unwin, London, 2nd ed., 1971.
VALENCY, MAURICE: *The Cart and the Trumpet*, Oxford University Press, New York, 1973.
The above books are most interesting on *The Devil's Disciple* while the following are informative or stimulating on Shaw's ideas in general.

TURCO, ALFRED: *Shaw's Moral Vision*, Cornell University Press, Ithaca, N.Y., 1976. Useful on the development of Shaw's philosophy and in particular on his debt to Ibsenism.

HUGO, LEON: *Bernard Shaw: Playwright and Preacher*, Methuen, London, 1971. Interesting on Shaw's theory of the life-force.

The author of these notes

EMELIE FITZGIBBON is a graduate of University College Cork in Ireland. She teaches English and Drama in that University and is one of the editors of the national theatre magazine, *Theatre Ireland*. Her previous publications include notes on Romantic Poetry and York Notes on Emily Dickinson. She is the regular theatre reviewer for *Books Ireland* and also writes for several other journals.

The first 250 titles